Reteach

Level 4

Teacher's Annotated Edition

A Division of The McGraw·Hill Companies

Columbus, Ohio

www.sra4kids.com

SRA/McGraw-Hill

A Division of The McGraw·Hill Companies

Send all inquiries to:
SRA/McGraw-Hill
8787 Orion Place
Columbus, OH 43240-4027

Printed in the United States of America.

ISBN 0-07-572030-2

5 6 7 8 9 POH 07 06 05

Table of Contents

►Cause and Effect

Focus Cause and effect relationships help readers understand why events happen in a certain way.

► A **cause** is why something happens.

► The **effect** is what happens as a result.

Cause	**Effect**
The boy kicked the ball →	The ball flew through the air.

Writers sometimes use signal words to show cause and effect relationships. Signal words, such as *because*, *so*, *if*, *then*, and *since*, help the reader know what happens and why it happens.

Practice Match each cause with its effect by drawing a line.

Cause

1. Cake batter is poured into a pan and placed into a hot oven.

2. An apple seed is planted.

3. Ice cubes and water are added to instant tea.

4. The bird flaps its wings.

5. A light switch on a wall is flipped up to the "on" position.

6. A musician places her lips on the mouthpiece and blows into the trumpet.

7. A bowling ball is rolled toward ten bowling pins.

Effect

a. An apple tree grows.

b. Iced tea is made.

c. A light is turned on.

d. A cake bakes.

e. Some bowling pins are knocked over.

f. The bird flies.

g. The trumpet makes a sound.

COMPREHENSION

▶**Cause and Effect**

Look at the following sentences. Some of the sentences show a cause and effect relationship. Others do not. Draw an X next to the sentences that show a cause and effect relationship. Look for signal words such as *since*, *if*, *so*, *then*, or *because*. Underline the signal words in the sentences that show cause and effect.

8. __X__ Because Jason threw a baseball at a front window of the house, the window broke.

9. _____ The cow jumped over the moon and bumped into a star.

10. _____ Spencer rode his bike to school and then to the library.

11. __X__ Since the lock was broken, the Johnsons no longer store their tools in the shed.

12. __X__ If the cookies are gone, then someone must have eaten them.

13. _____ The jacket belongs to Karen, who forgot it at the game.

14. __X__ The dog's house is empty, so she must be elsewhere.

15. __X__ I hear a bell ringing, so it must be the telephone.

16. _____ The computer is new, and is sitting on the student's desk.

17. __X__ Because it is raining, I will wear a raincoat.

18. _____ The cat usually attacked small animals.

19. __X__ If the book is not on the shelf, then someone has taken it.

Apply **Write an effect for the following cause.**

Because it is warm outdoors, **Answers will vary.** _____

COMPREHENSION

UNIT 1 **Risks and Consequences • Lesson 1** *Mrs. Frisby and the Crow*

▶ Short-Vowel Sounds

> The /a/ sound is in *lamb*.   The /e/ sound is in *hen*.
>
> The /i/ sound is in *pig*.   The /o/ sound is in *fox*.
>
> The /u/ sound is in *tug*.

Use these words to complete the exercise below.

rustic	shrubs	cactus	pasture	solid
victims	hundred	billion	traffic	tablet

Visualization Strategy Complete each word by filling in the missing short-vowel sound.

1. v_ctims   **victims**

2. r_stic   **rustic**

3. shr_bs   **shrubs**

4. s_lid   **solid**

5. h_ndred   **hundred**

6. c_ctus   **cactus**

7. p_sture   **pasture**

8. b_llion   **billion**

9. t_blet   **tablet**

10. tr_ffic   **traffic**

SPELLING

Unfamiliar Words

While reading the story "Mrs. Frisby and the Crow," you will come across words that are unfamiliar to you. There are several ways of finding the meanings of unfamiliar words.

Here are some hints to finding the meanings of words you do not understand:

▶Read the sentences around the word.

▶Try to learn the meaning of the word by reading the passage it is in.

▶Use a dictionary or thesaurus to find the meaning of unfamiliar words.

Practice   Use these words to complete the exercise below.

abreast	capacity	literally	dubiously	prospect

Complete each definition with a vocabulary word from the box. You may use a dictionary to help you complete this exercise.

1. next to each other; side by side __abreast__

2. the amount that can be held in a space __capacity__

3. something looked forward to; expected __prospect__

4. of doubtful promise; questionable __dubiously__

5. the truth; free from exaggeration __literally__

VOCABULARY

Name _____ Date _____

▶ **Nouns**

GRAMMAR AND USAGE

Rule	Example
▶A noun names a person, place, thing, or idea.	▶**barn, teacher, chair**
▶A common noun names any person, place, thing, or idea.	
▶A proper noun names a specific person, place, thing, or idea. Proper nouns are always capitalized.	▶**Ms. Carter, Mt. Rushmore, Liberty Bell**

Practice Read the paragraph and identify the nouns. Write five common nouns and five proper nouns on the lines below.

Some holidays in America remember our heroes. The man who explored the Americas, Christopher Columbus, and the man who won many victories for civil rights, Martin Luther King, Jr., are two heroes we honor every year. We celebrate the independence of our country on July 4th. Some holidays—Valentine's Day and April Fools' Day—are celebrated just for fun.

Answers will vary. Possible answers are shown.

Common nouns

1. holidays
2. heroes
3. man
4. victories
5. rights

Proper nouns

6. America
7. Americas
8. Christopher Columbus
9. Martin Luther King, Jr.
10. July

Point of View

In every story you read, a narrator tells the story from a certain point of view. A story may be told in **first-person point of view** or **third-person point of view**.

If the narrator takes part in the story's action, the story is written from **first-person point of view**. The narrator uses pronouns such as *I*, *me*, *my*, *we*, *us*, and *our* to tell the story.

If the narrator does *not* take part in the action, the story is written from a **third-person point of view**. The pronouns *he*, *she*, *they*, *them*, and *their* are used to tell the story.

Practice Read the sentences below. Tell whether each sentence is written using first-person *or* third-person point of view. Write your answers in the spaces provided. Remember to use pronouns as clues to the point of view.

1. Marcy and I went all the way around the track. __first-person__

2. The poodle walked past my dog like a queen walks past a speck of dust. __first-person__

3. His mom sent extra cookies for everyone on the team.
__third-person__

4. I was sure my teacher knew what I had done. __first-person__

5. Shelly and Claire sold their old toys at the yard sale. __third-person__

6. She smiled happily as she worked. __third-person__

7. The picture was our only clue. __first-person__

8. Stacey watched them run down the sidewalk. __third-person__

WRITER'S CRAFT

UNIT 1 Risks and Consequences • **Lesson 2** *Toto*

▶ Compare and Contrast

Focus To compare means telling how things are alike. To contrast means telling how things are different.

▶ To **compare** means telling how two or more things are alike.
   A triangle and a square are alike. They are both shapes.

▶ To **contrast** means telling how two or more things are different.
   A triangle and a square are different. A triangle has three sides.
   A square has four sides.

COMPREHENSION

Practice

▶ Look at the pairs of words. Write how they are alike in the spaces below. **Possible answers are shown.**

1. carrot   corn   Both are vegetables.

2. trumpet   guitar   Both are musical instruments.

3. car   bicycle Both have wheels.

4. cat   dog   Both are animals.

▶ Look at the pairs of words. Write how they are different in the spaces below. **Possible answers are shown.**

5. carrot   corn   A carrot is orange. Corn is yellow.

6. trumpet   guitar   You blow into a trumpet. You strum a guitar.

7. car   bicycle A car has an engine. A bicycle has pedals.

8. cat   dog   A cat meows. A dog barks.

UNIT I   Risks and Consequences • **Lesson 2** *Toto*

▶**Compare and Contrast**

▶Look at the pairs of words in the chart below. Write in the chart
how the words are alike and how they are different.
Answers will vary. Possible answers are shown.

Words	Alike	Different
chicken rabbit	**Both are animals.**	**A chicken has feathers. A rabbit has fur.**
tree flower	**Both are plants**	**A tree has a trunk. A flower has a stem.**
baseball basketball	**Both are sports.**	**In baseball, the ball is hit with a bat; in basketball, the ball is thrown through a hoop.**
fiction nonfiction	**Both can be read.**	**Fiction is not true, while nonfiction is true.**
pencil marker	**Both are things with which to write.**	**Writing from a pencil can be erased; writing from a marker cannot be erased.**

 **Think about two things you might compare and
contrast. Write the pair of things in the first column of
the chart below. In the second column, write how they
are alike. Write how they are different in the third
column. Answers will vary.**

Words	Alike	Different

COMPREHENSION

UNIT I Risks and Consequences • **Lesson 2** *Toto*

▶ The /ā/ Sound

> The /ā/ sound can be spelled *a*, *a_e*, *ai_*, *_ay*, and *eigh*.
>
> Examples: *favor*, *blaze*, *fail*, *play*, *eight*
>
> The *ay* spelling pattern is often found at the end of words or syllables.

 Consonant Substitution Strategy Use these words to complete the exercise below. Write the spelling words that are created by adding, dropping, or substituting one or more consonants.

stray	plains	claim	weigh	erase
bacon	brave	chamber	trail	sway

1. baton   **bacon**
2. rave   **brave**
3. frail   **trail**
4. neigh   **weigh**
5. trains   **plains**
6. tray   **stray**
7. eraser   **erase**
8. hamper   **chamber**
9. way   **sway**
10. aim   **claim**

SPELLING

Name _____ Date _____

▶Context Clues

A **context clue** is information within a sentence or nearby sentences that helps you learn the meaning of an unfamiliar word. If you know the meanings of the words around the unfamiliar word, you can begin to understand the meaning of the unfamiliar word.

Practice   **Use these words to complete the exercise below.**

ancestors	poachers	menacing	enviously	haughty

Complete each sentence with a vocabulary word.

1. Your parents and grandparents are among your
   _____**ancestors**_____.

2. The _____**haughty**_____ king refused to speak
   to common people.

3. After breaking my leg, I _____**enviously**_____
   watched as my classmates played basketball during
   recess.

4. _____**Poachers**_____ illegally hunt and capture
   wild animals.

5. The thought of rain was _____**menacing**_____ to
   the people at the outdoor picnic.

VOCABULARY

Name _____ Date _____

▶Plural and Possessive Nouns

Rule	**Example**
▶A **plural noun** names more than one person, place, thing, or idea. Most nouns become plural by adding *s* or *es* to the noun.	▶lamp, lamps, cat, cats
▶Some nouns become plural by changing spelling.	▶ox, oxen mouse, mice
▶Some nouns have the same spelling for singular and plural forms.	▶sheep, sheep ▶fish, fish
▶A **possessive noun** shows ownership. To show ownership, add *'s* to a singular noun that does not end in *s* or *es* (Mom's, children's), and add just *'* to a plural noun that ends in *s* or *es* (hikers', pictures').	

Practice

▶Write the plural form of each singular noun in the spaces below.

1. field   **fields**

2. loaf   **loaves**

3. woman   **women**

4. moss   **mosses**

5. child   **children**

▶Write two sentences about a pet you or a friend has. Use and underline possessive nouns.

Answers will vary.

_____

_____

Name _____ Date _____

 # Aim, Purpose, and Audience

> Before a writer begins any writing project, it is important to know exactly what his or her **aim**, **purpose**, and **audience** are.
>
> A writer's **aim** is the message he or she wants to convey. For example, if a writer writes a letter of complaint to a company, the writer's aim is probably to say he or she is disappointed about a product.
>
> A writer's **purpose** may be to inform, to explain, to entertain, or to persuade.
>
> The **audience** is the people who read a written product. Knowing who the audience is helps a writer make decisions about what words to use and how to say things.

Practice Read the following sentences or passages. For each sentence, answer the question that follows.
Answers will vary. Possible answers are shown.

1. I believe that the school's dress code is old-fashioned.

   What is this writer's purpose? __**to persuade**__

2. I wanted to stay in Berea, Kentucky, an extra day. In one shop, I watched a wood carver making beautiful little statues. In another, a potter was throwing pots on her wheel. The clay seemed to come to life under her hands.

   What is the writer's aim? __**To tell readers that Berea, Kentucky,**__

   __**is an interesting place to visit.**__

3. In this fairy tale, you will meet an old woman, a rabbit, and a fox. The old woman's name is Mia. The rabbit's name is Rabbit. And the fox's name is Fox.

   Who is the writer's audience? __**young children**__

WRITER'S CRAFT

UNIT I   Risks and Consequences • **Lesson 2** *Toto*

▶ Time and Order Words

WRITER'S CRAFT

> **Time and order** words tell when and in what order events happen.
>
> Here are the most common words that tell time and order.
>
> | after | before | finally | first | last | later |
> |---|---|---|---|---|---|
> | meanwhile | next | second | then | third | until |
>
> Writers use time and order words in many different kinds of writing. Here are some examples:
>
> ▶ a how-to book about sports or crafts or science experiments
>
> ▶ a story that involves a series of actions or events
>
> ▶ a history book that tells what happened and when
>
> Notice how the words that show order in the following paragraph make the instructions clear.
>
> Here's how to make my favorite sandwich. First, lay out two pieces of bread. Next, squirt mustard on each slice. Then lay some cheese on one slice and some bologna on the other. Finally, close the sandwich up, take a bite, and enjoy.

Practice   Underline the time and order words in each paragraph.

1. Before you read the story, look at the pictures. Then write what you think the story might be about. Finally, read the entire story.

2. Soon after that day, Janie ran into Michelle again. At first she wanted to go the other way. Then she decided to just say *hello*. Later, she was glad. Being friendly was better than running away.

3. First, read the instructions. Second, get the supplies you need. Third, do the experiment.

4. When we get to a campsite, everyone has a job. First, my dad checks in. Next, Mom chooses the best site. Then my sister gets fresh water while I collect firewood. And, last, Mom begins cooking dinner.

▶ Place and Location Words

Place and location words help readers understand where things are or where actions take place. Here are some common place and location words:

about	above	across	along	among	around
at	behind	beside	by	down	in, inside, into
near	on	out, outside	over	past	through
to	under	up	within	without	

In stories, writers use place and location words to help readers understand where characters are and what is happening.

Lou reached <u>into</u> his locker and pulled <u>out</u> his lunch. Other kids rushed <u>past</u> him. Suddenly, someone bumped <u>into</u> Lou's locker door. The door slammed <u>against</u> Lou's arm. His books landed <u>on</u> the floor with a bang. Worst of all, his lunch scattered <u>across</u> the floor <u>among</u> the rushing feet. Lou couldn't bear to look. *Squish!* That was the sound of a sandwich <u>under</u> a sneaker.

WRITER'S CRAFT

Practice Write the place or location word you see in each sentence.

1. Outside the window the birds ate the seeds. _____outside_____

2. Buses roared past us. _____past_____

3. We stayed inside our warm sleeping bags. _____inside_____

4. My markers were hiding under my notebook. _____under_____

5. Beyond the field is Mrs. Turner's house. _____beyond_____

6. Nell pushed against the gate. _____against_____

7. Along the way we read and slept. _____along_____

8. Frost on the window told us it was cold. _____on_____

9. No one knew what was behind us. _____behind_____

▶ Author's Point of View

COMPREHENSION

Focus Every story is told from a specific point of view that the author chooses. Point of view may be first-person or third-person.

In writing a story, the author creates a narrator who tells the story from a particular point of view.

▶ In a story told from the **first-person point of view,** the narrator is a character in the story. The narrator uses pronouns such as *I, me,* and *my* when telling the story.

▶ In a story told from the **third-person point of view,** the narrator is an outside observer looking at the happenings in the story. This narrator uses pronouns such as *he, she,* and *they* when telling the story.

Practice

▶ Look at the sentences below. In the spaces provided, write the point of view of each sentence. Remember, first-person point of view uses pronouns such as *I, me,* and *my*. Third-person point of view uses pronouns such as *he, she,* and *they.*

1. I ride my bicycle to school.   **first-person**

2. He is afraid of horses.   **third-person**

3. They enjoyed the movie.   **third-person**

4. Trevor gave the doll to me.   **first-person**

5. She practices the piano every day.   **third-person**

6. My mother baked cookies yesterday.   **first-person**

7. He is a member of the soccer team.   **third-person**

8. They love to sing and dance!   **third-person**

UNIT 1 **Risks and Consequences • Lesson 3** *Sarah, Plain and Tall*

▶**Author's Point of View**

▶Fill in the sentences below, using pronouns that show the first-person point of view. Use the pronouns *I, me,* and *my*.

9. These are the books that _____ **I** _____ like.

10. _____ **My** _____ father delivers mail in the neighborhood.

11. _____ **My** _____ baby sister looks like Grandma.

12. That belongs to _____ **me** _____.

▶Fill in the sentences below, using pronouns that show the third-person point of view. Use the pronouns *he, she,* and *they*.

13. _____ **She or He** _____ plays golf every Sunday afternoon.

14. _____ **They** _____ usually go to the museum together.

15. _____ **She** _____ is the mother of three children.

16. _____ **He or She** _____ is an architect.

▶Read the passage below. Then answer the questions.

Jerry's grandfather raises cattle on his farm. Jerry helps his grandfather take care of the animals and the crops. They sometimes see deer in the fields, and they enjoy the songs of the many different birds.

What is the point of view of the passage? _____ **third-person** _____

Write the word that tells you the point of view. _____ **they** _____

 Rewrite the following sentence, using the first-person point of view.

He helps his grandfather with the chores.

I help my grandfather with the chores.

_____

UNIT 1 **Risks and Consequences • Lesson 3** *Sarah, Plain and Tall*

▶ The /ē/ Sound

The /ē/ sound can be spelled *ee*, *ea*, *_ie_*, and *_ey*.

Examples: *speech, deal, weight, monkey*

When two vowels come together, the first vowel is usually long. *(peal)*

The *_ey* spelling of the /ē/ sound is always at the end of a word.

Use these words to complete the exercise below.

seals	prairie	wreath	hockey	trolley
seaweed	donkey	sneak	married	yield

 Proofreading Strategy Circle the misspelled words and write the correct spelling on the lines provided.

1. (Seels) are mammals that have flippers instead of feet. **seals** _____

2. A (dunkey) resembles a horse. **donkey** _____

3. There was (seawied) in the water. **seaweed** _____

4. A (prairey) dog is a small, plump animal with a short tail and a grayish brown coat. **prairie** _____

5. The game of (hockie) requires two teams of six players each. **hockey** _____

6. The cat would (sneek) up on a toy before pouncing on it. **sneak** _____

7. You can buy a (wreth) of flowers from a flower shop. **wreath** _____

8. A (trolly) resembles a train, but it rides on a street. **trolley** _____

9. The couple got (marreed) on a warm day in July. **married** _____

10. The farm's (yild) of corn was greater this year than last year. **yield** _____

SPELLING

Name _____ Date _____

▶Word Structure

A **compound word** is a word made up of two or more smaller words (*raincoat*).

A **prefix** is an addition to the beginning of a word.
The prefix *re-* means "again." The prefix *un-* means "not or reverse."

A **suffix** is an addition to the end of a word.
The suffix *-less* means "without."

Root words are words to which a prefix and or suffix can be added.

The following roots mean:

curl—to form into a curved (ring) shape

shingle—building materials used to cover the roof or sides of a building

home—the place where you live

shuffle—to move around

VOCABULARY

Practice

▶ Use the information provided in the box to write the meanings of the following words.

1. reshingle __to put the building or roof back together, using shingles__

2. reshuffle __to move around again__

3. uncurl __to remove from a curved (ring) shape__

4. homeless __without a place to live__

▶ Break the compound word into two smaller words.

5. hearthstones __hearth•stones__

UNIT 1 Risks and Consequences • **Lesson 3** *Sarah, Plain and Tall*

▶Pronouns

GRAMMAR AND USAGE

Rule	**Example**
▶A **pronoun** is used in place of one or more nouns.	▶President Bush said **President Bush** would speak at the university. President Bush said **he** would speak at the university. ▶**Sam and Jamie** met him in Washington, D.C. **They** met him in Washington, D.C.
▶When you speak of yourself and someone else, always speak of yourself last.	▶**Serena and I** are going to hear President Bush speak.

Practice

▶**Underline the pronouns in these sentences.**

1. <u>You</u> would enjoy learning about the pony express.

2. <u>It</u> was started in 1860.

3. A group of men said that <u>they</u> would deliver mail to the West.

4. <u>Their</u> horseback riders would hand off the mail to another rider.

5. <u>He</u> would then continue the route.

▶**Circle the correct combination.**

6. (Sunee and I, I and Sunee) went to the museum today.

7. Chet met (me and Sunee, Sunee and me) at the dinosaur exhibit.

Name _____ Date _____

▶ Topic Sentences

A **topic sentence** states the main idea of a paragraph. In many paragraphs, the topic sentence is the first sentence. However, a topic sentence may be anywhere in the paragraph.

Here are three things to remember about a topic sentence. A topic sentence should:

1. tell what the paragraph is about.
2. grab readers' attention and make them want to keep reading.
3. state an idea narrow enough to be covered in one paragraph.

Example

Amanda is the best detective I know. She's the one who solved the mystery of Mrs. Sharda's disappearing chalk. The door in Mrs. Sharda's room has a habit of slamming. When it does, the chalk falls off the chalk rail onto the floor. At night, the cleaning crew does its job and sweeps the chalk away. That's why Mrs. Sharda has to get new chalk every morning. Only Amanda could have figured that out.

Practice Following each group of sentences are two possible topic sentences. Write the letter of the topic sentence that best fits the group of sentences in the space provided.

1. They learned how to grow corn, squash, and beans. The boys learned how to weave beautiful designs into cloth. Fathers also taught their sons to paint designs on pottery. **a**_____

   a. Pueblo boys learned many things from their fathers.
   b. The Pueblos lived in the deserts of the West and Southwest.

2. They need only a little shelter in which to make a nest. They like window ledges and spots up under the eaves of buildings. Loud noises, such as traffic noises, don't bother pigeons. **b**_____

   a. Pigeons are pests that should be removed from our cities.
   b. Pigeons are good at living in the city.

WRITER'S CRAFT

Name _____ Date _____

 # Paragraph Form

Most **paragraphs** are groups of at least two sentences that tell about the same thing. The first sentence of a paragraph is indented.

A paragraph has to have a main idea. That idea is stated in a topic sentence. The topic sentence is often the first sentence in a paragraph. However, the topic sentence *may* be anywhere in the paragraph.

Other sentences give details that support, or tell more about, the main idea.

Example

On Fun Fridays we visit other classrooms and learn about all kinds of things. Two weeks ago I helped build a model of the Great Wall of China. Did you know it is the largest human-made object on Earth? Last week, I made a fossil using plaster of paris and a pine branch. Of course, a real fossil takes millions of years to form.

Practice **Read each paragraph. Then answer the questions that follow.**

1.   Marlin is the best little brother in the world. He doesn't follow me around. He almost never snoops in my room. And whenever he doesn't like his lunch, he gives it to me because he knows I'm always hungry.

What is the topic sentence of this paragraph?

Marlin is the best little brother in the world.

2.   The dim attic was full of marvelous things. The big black trunks especially interested me. One, I knew, was full of clothes. They were huge clothes. The light from the one attic window made me squint. Another trunk was full of old magazines.

Which sentence in this paragraph does *not* tell about the main idea?

The light from the one attic window made me squint.

WRITER'S CRAFT

Name _____ Date _____

▶ Staying on Topic

Staying on topic means picking one idea and sticking with it. In a paragraph, include information only about the main idea. Don't use extra words. And do not include thoughts or ideas that don't relate to the main idea.

How do you know if you're staying on topic? When you look at the first draft of a piece of writing, make sure *you* know what the main idea of each paragraph is. Then look at each sentence and ask yourself, "Does this sentence tell more about the main idea, or does it talk about something else?"

Staying on topic helps keep your readers interested in what you have to say.

Practice — **Each of the following paragraphs contains a sentence that is not on topic. Find the sentence and write it in the space following the paragraph.**

1.　　I hate to complain, but being left-handed is tough sometimes. Most of the scissors at school don't work for me. When we learned cursive writing last year I got so confused. I was the only lefty in the class. Mary Osborn, on the other hand, has beautiful cursive writing.

Mary Osborn, on the other hand, has beautiful cursive

writing.

2.　　The library has a place for everyone. Upstairs, gray-haired men read newspapers and news magazines. Quiet college students sit at tables with stacks of books. I never go up to that floor. On the main floor, grown-ups search the shelves for the books they need. Downstairs, a wide-open room is full of low shelves and lots of soft chairs. Children and parents read together in the chairs.

I never go up to that floor.

COMPREHENSION

▶ Sequence

Focus Sequence is the order in which things happen in a story. A writer uses time and order words to help the reader follow the sequence in a story.

▶ **Order words** show the order in which things take place. Words such as *first, then, next,* and *finally* show order.

▶ **Time words** show how time passes in a story. Words such as *spring, tomorrow,* and *morning* show time.

Practice

▶ Look at the pictures. Put the pictures in the proper sequence. Write the correct order word in the space below each picture. Use the order words *first, then,* and *finally*.

then
_____

first
_____

finally
_____

UNIT 1 Risks and Consequences • **Lesson 4** *Escape*

▶**Sequence**

▶ Look at the following sentences about "Escape." Put the sentences in the proper sequence. Write the correct order word in front of the sentence. Use the order words *first*, *next*, and *finally*.

1. **Next** _____ Homer, Lurvy, and the cocker spaniel chase Wilbur around the yard.

2. **Finally** _____ Wilbur eats the slops, happy to be home again.

3. **First** _____ Wilbur squeezes through the fence and is standing in the yard.

▶ Look at the following sentences. Complete each sentence by filling in a time word. Use the time words in the box below.

soon	winter	afternoon
summer	yesterday	morning

Answers may vary.

4. I will eat breakfast in the **morning** _____.

5. Ken walked to the park **yesterday** _____.

6. Lunch is usually served in the **afternoon** _____.

7. **Soon** _____ it will be Christmas.

8. The big snowstorm in New York happened last **winter** _____.

9. During the **summer** _____, it gets very hot in Texas.

10. We will visit Uncle Bob **soon** _____.

Answers will vary. Possible answer is shown.
Write the first sentence of the following sequence. Use an order word in your sentence.

First, I will take the ticket out of my pocket.
_____

Next, I will give the flight attendant my ticket. Finally, I will board the airplane.

▶ The /ō/ Sound

The /ō/ sound can be spelled *o*, *o_e*, *oa_*, and *_ow*.

Examples: *only, grove, goal, hollow*

When two vowels come together, the first one is always long *(moan)*. The *e* at the end of a word is always silent; this makes the vowel before it long *(stone)*.

Use these words to complete the exercise below.

coax	bowl	shadow	over	cobra
groan	coast	elbow	narrow	whole

 Visualization Strategy Complete the spelling words by filling in the missing letters.

1. gr_ _ n   **groan**

2. c_ _st   **coast**

3. c_ _x   **coax**

4. b_ _ l   **bowl**

5. narr_ _   **narrow**

6. wh_le   **whole**

7. shad_ _   **shadow**

8. _ver   **over**

9. el_ _ w   **elbow**

10. c_ bra   **cobra**

UNIT I Risks and Consequences • **Lesson 4** *Escape*

▶Dictionary

You can learn many things from a dictionary, such as:
1. The definition or definitions of a word.
2. How a word is broken into syllables.
3. How to pronounce a word.

Use your dictionary to complete the following exercises.

Practice

▶ **Use a dictionary to break each word into syllables.**

1. perspiration   **per•spi•ra•tion**

2. trough   **trough**

3. asparagus   **as•par•a•gus**

4. scythes   **scythes**

5. reconsider   **re•con•sid•er**

▶ **Write each vocabulary word next to its pronunciation code.**

6. ə 'spar ə gəs   **asparagus**

7. rē kən 'si dər   **reconsider**

8. 'trō   **trough**

9. 'sīthz   **scythes**

10. pər spə 'rā shən   **perspiration**

VOCABULARY

▶Verbs

GRAMMAR AND USAGE

Rule	**Example**
▶ A **verb** is a word that shows an action or expresses a state of being. An action verb shows what the subject does.	▶ Angela **danced** in the school program.
▶ A **linking verb** renames or describes the subject.	▶ My sister **is** a great soccer player. Our new car **is** red.
▶ A **helping verb** helps the main verb.	▶ I **will** read the book tonight.

Practice

▶ **Circle the action verbs in the paragraph.**

The Silk Road (got) its name from the Chinese silk (carried) from China to Persia. The silk then (made) its long journey to Europe. Few traders (traveled) the entire Silk Road.

▶ **Look at the underlined verb in each sentence. Write *L* if the verb is a linking verb. Write *H* if the verb is a helping verb.**

1. You <u>are</u> interested in science. **L** _____

2. Air <u>is</u> fascinating to study. **L** _____

3. There <u>are</u> many gases in air. **L** _____

4. No one <u>has</u> seen air. **H** _____

UNIT I Risks and Consequences • **Lesson 4** *Escape*

▶Thesis Sentence

A **thesis sentence** states the main idea of an entire paper. The thesis sentence is usually the first sentence in the first paragraph of a text. However, a thesis sentence may be anywhere in the paragraph.

Here are three things to remember about a thesis sentence. A thesis sentence should:

1. tell what the entire piece is about.
2. grab readers' attention and make them want to keep reading.
3. state an idea that can be covered in the paper.

Example

The doctor's waiting room is always a busy place. Behind a big sliding glass window, the staff answer phones and talk among themselves. In the waiting room itself, there is always at least one crying baby. People try not to stare at the baby's poor parents who are trying to quiet the baby. Other people flip through magazines. Over in the corner, a woman reads a story to her children.

WRITER'S CRAFT

Practice Following each group of sentences are two possible thesis sentences. Write the letter of the sentence that best tells what the group of sentences is about in the space provided.

1. Many vegetable plants have flowers, but they are not very showy. And others, such as corn and carrots, don't have any flowers at all. **a** _____

   a. Some flowers add a nice touch in a vegetable garden.
   b. Planting flowers in a garden helps the vegetables grow.

2. I know that in real life, colds aren't such a big deal. But when you have a cold, it's a big deal. What made this one so bad is that I was so stuffed up. My head felt like a huge pillow. I was afraid to stand up for fear I'd tip over. **b** _____

   a. Having a cold can be awful.
   b. I just had the worst cold of my life.

▶ Supporting Details

Different kinds of writing require different kinds of **supporting details**. For example, a paragraph in a piece of persuasive writing might require reasons or facts.

Example

    Our school is too crowded. This year, 428 students are enrolled. The original building plan for the school states that its capacity is 340 students. The building has not grown since then. The teachers' lunch room has become a classroom, and so has the locker room.

In a story, a paragraph's main idea is likely to be supported by descriptive details.

Example

    We felt like cookies baking in an oven. Even the shade seemed so hot we could hardly breathe. We felt puffy and sweaty. And all we wanted to do was sit still and try not to be hot.

WRITER'S CRAFT

Practice **Read the paragraph below. Then follow the directions.**

    In one story, Dr. Herriot is called to trim a pet bird's beak. He reaches into the cage and takes hold of the bird. The frightened bird dies in his hand. The bird's owner, a very old woman, does not see or hear well. Instead of telling the woman and breaking her heart, Herriot gets a new bird for her. She never knows the difference.

List two supporting details from this paragraph.

Accept any sentences except the first.

_____

_____

_____

_____

UNIT I Risks and Consequences • **Lesson 4** *Escape*

▶ Order of Paragraphs

When you write to inform, your work should include three parts.

▶ **Introduction:** The writer tells what the report is about and catches readers' interest.

▶ **Body:** The writer presents most of the information in a logical manner. The body is usually the longest part of a report.

▶ **Conclusion:** The writer ties together his or her ideas. The conclusion may contain a summary of those ideas, but it should not simply repeat the ideas.

Practice Read the report below. Then answer the questions that follow.

Old stories can still teach us things. Consider the story of King Midas. One of the Greek gods gave Midas the power to turn everything he touched into gold. At first, the greedy Midas was thrilled. Soon, his power caused trouble. Midas's food turned to gold, and he could not eat. Then he turned his beloved daughter to gold. Finally, Midas knew that having this power was not a good thing.

In the end, the Greek god told Midas to bathe in a certain river. By doing so, he washed away his golden touch. The lesson his story teaches about greed is at least as important now as it was in ancient Greece.

1. In the introductory paragraph, which sentence states the main idea?

   Old stories can still teach us things.

2. What sentence in the conclusion restates or summarizes the main idea?

   The lesson his story teaches about greed is at least as

   important now as it was in ancient Greece.

WRITER'S CRAFT

COMPREHENSION

▶ Main Idea and Details

Focus The main idea is what a paragraph is about. Details in the paragraph support the main idea.

A paragraph has a main idea and details that support the main idea.

▶ The **main idea** is the most important point the writer makes. The main idea is often stated in a clear topic sentence. The topic sentence is usually at the beginning or at the end of a paragraph.

▶ The other sentences in a paragraph have **details**, or information, that describe the main idea more fully.

Practice Look at the main ideas and details. Write an *X* next to the sentence that describes the main idea more fully.

1. Main idea: As a child, Mae dreamed of being a scientist.

   __X__ She loved working on science projects in school.

   _____ She took dancing lessons.

   _____ She helped her mother cook dinner after school.

2. Main idea: Trevor loves animals.

   _____ He walks to school every morning.

   _____ He loves chocolate ice cream.

   __X__ He works with his father at the animal shelter.

3. Main idea: Mother grows vegetables in her garden.

   __X__ She grows cucumbers.

   _____ She is a doctor.

   _____ Earthworms are slimy!

Name _____ Date _____

▶ **Main Idea and Details**

Read the following paragraph, and answer the questions.

Over the years, Girl Scouting has become very popular in the United States. Juliette Gordon Low started the Girl Scouts of the U.S.A. in 1912. When she died in 1927, there were more than 160,000 Girl Scouts in the United States. Today, millions of girls belong to Girl Scout troops across the nation. **Answers will vary. Possible answers are shown.**

4. What is this paragraph about? Write the sentence that contains the main idea. **Over the years, Girl Scouting has become very popular in the United States.**

5. Now look for sentences with details that support the main idea. Write one sentence that contains details that describe the main idea more fully. **When she died in 1927, there were more than 160,000 Girl Scouts in the United States.**

Look at the following paragraph. The main idea is missing. Figure out the main idea from the details in the sentences. Then, write the main idea on the lines below. **Answers will vary. Possible answer is shown.**

Vanilla is my mother's favorite flavor. My little sister loves strawberry ice cream. Dad usually gets banana ice cream. My favorite flavor is chocolate.

Everyone in my family has a different favorite flavor of ice cream.

Name _____ Date _____

▶ The /ī/ Sound

SPELLING

> The /ī/ sound can be spelled *i*, *i_e*, *igh*, and *_y*.
>
> Examples: *mild, glide, high, type*
>
> The /ī/ sound is usually spelled *i* and *i_e* in the middle of a word (*mild, glide*).

knight	rhyme	pilot	supply	icicle
wired	pirate	style	science	skylight

 Proofreading Strategy Circle the misspelled words in the sentences, then write the correct spelling on the lines provided.

1. An airline (pielot) uses instruments to fly a plane. __pilot__

2. A (pyrate) is a person who robs ships at sea. __pirate__

3. In Great Britain, a (knite) should be addressed as "sir." __knight__

4. Words that (rhime) often sound alike. __rhyme__

5. Fashion magazines show clothes in the latest (stile). __style__

6. A (skylite) is a window in a ceiling or roof. __skylight__

7. The (supplie) of water for a city may come from a reservoir. __supply__

8. An (icecle) is formed by water that freezes as it drips. __icicle__

9. We can learn about things in nature and the universe through (sceince). __science__

10. I (wiered) the broken gate back together. __wired__

The /ī/ Sound • Reteach

▶ **Thesaurus**

A **thesaurus** is a tool that can help you learn the meaning of a word by listing the synonyms for the word. Like the words in a dictionary, the words in a thesaurus are placed in alphabetical order.

A **synonym** is a word that has the same, or close to the same, meaning as another word.

> *happy* is a synonym for *glad*

Both words have the same basic meaning. Knowing that happy and glad are synonyms can help you understand that their meanings are the same.

Practice Use these words to complete the exercise below.

astronaut	orbit	gravity	satellite	laboratories

Replace the underlined word in the sentence with a vocabulary word.

1. It takes 365 days for Earth to <u>move around</u> the sun. __**orbit**__

2. A <u>man-made moon</u> is used to provide information about conditions in space. __**satellite**__

3. <u>Force</u> pulls things toward the center of Earth. __**gravity**__

4. Mae Jemison was a <u>space traveler</u>. __**astronaut**__

5. Scientists conduct their experiments in <u>testing rooms</u>. __**laboratories**__

VOCABULARY

Name _____ Date _____

▶What Is a Sentence?

GRAMMAR AND USAGE

Rule	Example
▶ A **sentence** has two parts—a subject and a predicate. The **subject** of a sentence tells who or what the sentence is about.	▶ **Caleb** called his mother. **Happiness** is an emotion.
▶ The **predicate** of a sentence tells something about the subject.	▶ Jose **walked down the street**.

Practice Complete the sentences in the chart below with a subject or predicate from the box.

a salmon run   a time line   is a book of facts   is in Asia

Subject	Predicate
A time line	shows events in the order they happened.
A salmon run	is the yearly return of salmon to lay eggs in freshwater rivers.
An almanac	**is a book of facts.**
China	**is in Asia.**

UNIT I Risks and Consequences • **Lesson 5** *Mae Jemison: Space Scientist*

▶Exact Words

Exact words are words that name *specific* people, places, things, or actions. Writers use exact words to make their writing more interesting. General words may tell about a person, place, or event, but exact words create a picture of a person, place, or event.

In the first column below are some general words. In the second column are some exact words that you could use to replace the general words.

ball	baseball, rubber ball, football
walk	shuffle, pace, march, tromp
big	huge, giant, broad, vast

If you need ideas for exact words, look up a general word in a thesaurus. The thesaurus will give you many choices from which to choose.

WRITER'S CRAFT

Practice Each sentence below contains a general word in italic type. Replace the general words with exact words to improve each sentence.
Possible answers are shown.

1. Gail *looked* out the window.

Gail stared out the window.

2. The mouse nibbled on the *fruit.*

The mouse nibbled on an apple.

3. The *man* crossed the street.

The police officer crossed the street.

4. Neil *walked* across the yard.

Neil marched across the yard.

► **WRITER'S CRAFT**

► Effective Beginnings and Endings

> The **beginning** of a story or article is where a reader decides whether to keep reading, or whether to stop.
>
> Here are some techniques for writing effective beginnings.
> - ► Give a vivid description.
> - ► Introduce a problem.
> - ► Use dialogue.
>
> For an article, these techniques create effective beginnings.
> - ► Ask a question.
> - ► Tell about a problem.
> - ► Use an anecdote, or personal story.
>
> The **ending** of a story or article is also important. At the end of a story, the characters' problems need to be solved.
>
> In an article, the ending should summarize the article's main idea. A good ending leaves readers with something to think about.

Practice Make a check mark on the space in front of each effective beginning or ending. If a beginning or ending passage needs improvement, make changes and write your new version.
Possible revisions are given.

1. _____ Do you want to know about snails?

   Have you ever wondered how a snail gets into its shell?

   _____

2. ✓_____ Finally, the results of the survey show that students do require a full four minutes to get from the west wing of the building to the gymnasium.

   _____

   _____

Name _____ Date _____

 # Telling in Time Order

Writers often tell about events in the order in which they happened. To help readers follow along, writers use signal words.

Signal words that tell when something happened are called time words. Signal words that show the order in which things happened are called order words. Here are some examples of time and order signal words.

Time Words	**Order Words**
yesterday, afternoon	first, then, later, meanwhile
winter	after
at 3:00, April	while, finally

Practice   Complete each sentence by filling in a signal word that shows time. Use the signal words in the box below.

after	afternoon	finally	midnight	month
morning	soon	tomorrow	winter	yesterday

1. I will eat a good breakfast in the _____ **morning** _____.

2. School gets out in the _____ **afternoon** _____.

3. _____ **Yesterday** _____ I met Ken in the park.

4. There was a huge snowstorm in the _____ **winter** _____ of 1978.

5. I hope my grandparents arrive _____ **soon** _____.

6. Maybe the letter I am expecting will come _____ **tomorrow** _____ or the next day.

7. Just last _____ **month** _____ it seemed hot, but now it is cool autumn.

WRITER'S CRAFT

▶ Drawing Conclusions

COMPREHENSION

Focus Drawing conclusions helps readers get more information from a story.

Here is how you **draw conclusions**.

▶ Look for bits of information, or details, about a character or an event in a story. Use these details to make a statement or draw a conclusion about that character or event.

▶ Sometimes the conclusion is already stated in a sentence in the story.

Practice

▶ Look at the groups of sentences below. The sentences in the first column are details. The sentences in the second column are possible conclusions. One conclusion is correct, and one is incorrect. Put an *X* next to the sentence that could be the conclusion to the first pair of sentences. The first one is done for you.

Details

Conclusions

1. Brad likes fruit.

Apples are fruit.

____ Brad hates apples.

X Brad likes apples.

2. Connor loves animals.

Dogs are animals.

X Connor loves dogs.

____ Dogs love animals.

3. Samantha likes outdoor sports.

Soccer is an outdoor sport.

____ Samantha does not like soccer.

X Samantha likes soccer.

4. Ten pennies equal ten cents.

One dime equals ten cents.

____ One dime is worth more than ten pennies.

X Ten pennies equal one dime.

UNIT I **Risks and Consequences • Lesson 6** *Two Tickets to Freedom*

▶**Drawing Conclusions**

▶**Read the paragraph. Then answer the following.**

Mrs. Golding put a soup bone on a dish. Planning to make soup later, she put the dish on the counter in the kitchen. Grover, her dog, was watching her closely. He would take the bone when given a chance. The front doorbell rang. Mrs. Golding left the kitchen to answer the door. When she walked back into the kitchen, both the dog and the bone were gone.

Answers may vary. Possible answers are shown.

5. The sentences in this paragraph contain many details. One detail tells that Grover watched Mrs. Golding closely. Write two more details you find in this paragraph.

Detail: __**Mrs. Golding placed a soup bone in a dish on**__ __**the counter.**__

Detail: __**The doorbell rang and Mrs. Golding left the room.**__

6. From the details in this paragraph, what can you conclude?

__**The dog jumped onto the counter and took the bone.**__

 **Apply** Read the following pairs of statements, and draw a conclusion. Write your sentences in the spaces below.

All goats are animals.
Gordon is a goat.

Conclusion: __**Gordon is an animal.**__

A biography is nonfiction.
"Two Tickets to Freedom" is a biography.

Conclusion: __**"Two Tickets to Freedom" is nonfiction.**__

COMPREHENSION

▶ The /o͞o/ and /ū/ Sounds

SPELLING

The /o͞o/ sound can be spelled *o_e, u_e, _ue, _ew, oo,* and *ui.*

Examples: *dew, foot, loose, fruit, juice, prove*

The /ū/ sound can be spelled *_ew, _ue,* and *u_e.*

Examples: *few, hue, use*

Use these words to complete the exercise below.

proof	value	whose	cue	crew
issue	boost	truce	lose	flute

Consonant Substitution Strategy Write the spelling words that are created by adding, dropping, or substituting one or more consonants.

1. whole   **whose**

2. lost   **lose**

3. tissue   **issue**

4. shrew   **crew**

5. roof   **proof**

6. salute   **value**

7. roost   **boost**

8. fluke   **flute**

9. spruce   **truce**

10. hue   **cue**

▶Context Clues

A **context clue** is information within a sentence or nearby sentences that helps you learn the meaning of an unfamiliar word. If you know the meanings of the words around the unfamiliar word, you can begin to understand the meaning of the unfamiliar word.

Practice   Write the meaning of the underlined word in the sentence.

1. The people lost their <u>liberty</u> under the rule of the unfair king.

    to act, think, or speak the way you please

2. The wind <u>agitated</u> the water and made waves.

    to shake or stir up

3. We tried to <u>console</u> the loser.

    to comfort

4. The <u>abolitionist</u> worked very hard to free the slaves.

    a person who was in favor of ending slavery

5. Look at the <u>predicament</u> you're in because you accepted two invitations for the same evening.

    a difficult situation

VOCABULARY

▶ Kinds of Sentences

GRAMMAR AND USAGE

Rule	Example
▶ A **declarative** sentence makes a statement and ends with a period.	▶ George Washington was our first president.
▶ An **interrogative** sentence asks a question and ends with a question mark.	▶ Have you been to his home at Mount Vernon?
▶ An **imperative** sentence makes a request or gives a command and usually ends with a period.	▶ Visit there if you get the opportunity.
▶ An **exclamatory** sentence expresses strong feeling and ends with an exclamation point.	▶ What a great experience it will be!

Practice Look at the sentences below. Write *D* next to each declarative sentence, *Q* next to each question, *I* next to each imperative sentence, and *E* next to each exclamatory sentence.

1. What is your favorite subject? **Q** _____

2. Mae was not discouraged. **D** _____

3. What a wonderful surprise! **E** _____

4. Get a ticket at the window. **I** _____

5. She has read many science books. **D** _____

6. What is your last name? **Q** _____

Name _____ Date _____

 # Making Inferences

Focus Making inferences helps a reader understand the total picture in a story.

An **inference** is a statement you make about a character or an event in a story when you read.

Here is what you use to make an inference.

▶ First, use **information** from the story. Facts and descriptions in a story are types of information you can use to make an inference.

▶ Combine the information from the story with your **personal experience** or knowledge to make an inference.

Practice Read the paragraph below. Then answer the following questions.

The day that Ted broke his arm started out like most days. He struggled out of bed and ate breakfast. Then he looked at the kitchen clock. He had only three minutes to get to the bus stop! Ted grabbed his bookbag and flew out the door. He wished he had seen the family's dog standing outside the door. He tripped over her and landed on the wooden steps. The rest of the story is too painful to tell!

Possible answers are shown.

A fact is information you can use to make an inference. In the paragraph above, one fact is that Ted runs out the door to catch the bus. Write another fact from the passage.

Ted broke his arm.

_____

Make an inference based on the above paragraph. Remember, an inference is a statement about characters or events in a story. To make an inference, use the information from the story and your personal knowledge and experience. Write your inference here.

Ted broke his arm by tripping over the dog.

_____

COMPREHENSION

UNIT 1 Risks and Consequences • **Lesson 7** *Daedalus and Icarus*

▶**Making Inferences**

Read the following paragraphs. Think about the information in each paragraph and your personal knowledge or experience. Then complete each inference below with the correct word.

The sky was gray. It was a cold day that Thursday morning in November. The children were excited. Soon, they would be on their way to their grandmother's house. They could not help but think of the special dinner they would eat, including turkey, mashed potatoes, and stuffing. Grandmother always had the best desserts, too.

Inference: The children are going to their grandmother's house to celebrate **Thanksgiving** _____.

"Aha! Here it is!" Ben exclaimed.

He had been looking for his pet's leash for hours. Ben chuckled as he pulled the leash from under the sofa. He also found a rubber bone and an old shoe Snooper loved to chew.

"Snooper is very, very smart," Ben said to himself. Snooper probably hid the leash because he did not want to see Dr. Watson. Snooper hated getting shots and did not care for Dr. Watson.

Inference: Snooper is what type of animal? **a dog** _____

 Make another inference from the passage about Ben and Snooper. Write your statement here.

Answers will vary. _____

_____

COMPREHENSION

Making Inferences • Reteach

UNIT 1 Risks and Consequences • **Lesson 7** *Daedalus and Icarus*

▶Review

> The /ā/ sound can be spelled *a*, *a_e*, *ai_*, *_ay*, and *eigh*.
>
> The /ē/ sound can be spelled *ee*, *ea*, *_ie_*, and *_ey*.
>
> The /ō/ sound can be spelled *o*, *o_e*, *oa_*, and *_ow*.
>
> The /ī/ sound can be spelled *i*, *i_e*, *igh*, and *_y*.

Visualization Strategy Identify the highlighted vowels in the words as long or short. The first one is done for you.

1. chamber   *Long a*
2. lamp   /a/
3. clock   /o/
4. swallow   /ŏ/
5. crash   /a/
6. brain   /ā/
7. deck   /e/
8. erase   /ā/
9. film   /i/
10. shadow   /ō/

11. fed   /e/
12. creature   /ē/
13. seaweed   /ē/
14. dusk   /u/
15. style   /ī/
16. pick   /i/
17. spite   /ī/
18. thump   /u/
19. neighbor   /ā/
20. grip   /i/

SPELLING

UNIT I Risks and Consequences • **Lesson 7** *Daedalus and Icarus*

Dictionary and Thesaurus

VOCABULARY

> A **dictionary** uses a sentence or phrase to define a word.
>
> A **thesaurus** uses synonyms to define a word. A thesaurus can also be used to find new ways of saying things.
>
> Thesaurus Definition
>
> **delectable**—delicious, tasty, enjoyable
>
> **luxurious**—rich, splendid
>
> **hurtle**—rush, race, speed
>
> **daubed**—smeared, plastered
>
> **vault**—roof, ceiling

Complete each sentence with a word from the box.

1. The ball __hurtled__ toward the net.

2. We stayed in a __luxurious__ hotel during our vacation.

3. There was paint __daubed__ on the walls of the building.

4. The __vault__ of the tunnel curved up into darkness.

5. The cake we bought from the bakery was __delectable__.

▶Review

▶Nouns/Plural and Possessive Nouns/Pronouns

Write above each underlined word whether it is a noun
(N), a plural noun (PL), a possessive noun (PO), or a
pronoun (P).

                 N   **P**
      Look at the <u>person</u> next to <u>you</u>. Although each
N   **N**
<u>person</u> is dressed differently, every <u>person</u> is wearing
          N   **N**   **N**   **PO**   **N**
the same <u>thing</u>—<u>skin</u>. <u>Skin</u> is the <u>body's</u> largest <u>organ</u>.
P **N**   **P** **PL**   **PL**   **P**
<u>Our</u> <u>skin</u> protects <u>our</u> <u>bodies</u> from <u>germs</u> and gives <u>us</u>
     N   **N**   **P**   **N**
the <u>sense</u> of <u>touch</u>. And <u>it</u> lasts a <u>lifetime</u>!

▶Verbs/What Is a Sentence?

Circle the verbs in these sentences. Underline the subject
once, and underline the predicate twice.

1. <u>Animals</u> (use) <u>a variety of actions to protect themselves.</u>

2. <u>The parent</u> (flies) <u>away to safety.</u>

▶Kinds of Sentences

Write the type of sentence–declarative, interrogative,
imperative, or exclamatory–in the space provided. Add the
correct end punctuation.

3. _____**interrogative**_____ Do you know how to swim **?**_____

4. _____**imperative**_____ Come to the swim tournament with me **.**_____

5. _____**exclamatory**_____ What an exciting experience it will be **!**_____

GRAMMAR AND USAGE

Dollars and Sense • Lesson I *Starting a Business*

▶ Main Idea and Details

Focus

The main idea is what a paragraph is about. Details in the paragraph support the main idea.

A paragraph has a main idea and details that support the main idea.

▶ The **main idea** is the most important point the writer makes. The main idea is often stated in a clear topic sentence. The topic sentence is usually at the beginning or the end of a paragraph.

▶ The other sentences in a paragraph have **details,** or information, that describe the main idea more fully.

Practice

Look at the main idea and details. Write an *X* next to the sentence that more fully describes the main idea.

1. Main idea: A time line shows the order in which things happen.

   __X__ The thing that happened first is always on the left.

   _____ I started the time line with 1970.

   _____ A time line can be fun to make.

2. Main idea: The first colonists came from Spain.

   _____ A fort would be a good thing for a new colony.

   _____ Christopher Columbus traveled in three ships from Spain.

   __X__ They built a colony called St. Augustine.

COMPREHENSION

UNIT 2 Dollars and Sense • **Lesson 1** *Starting a Business*

▶ **Reteach: Main Idea and Details**

 **Read the following paragraph. Then answer the questions below.**

Answers will vary. Possible answers are shown.

Ice hockey is one of the fastest of all team sports. Its players race across the rink on ice skates. They swing their sticks to knock a hard rubber puck into the other team's goal. Hockey players are constantly on the move. The game does not stop even when players are substituted. The speed of play results in plenty of rough-and-tumble action.

3. What is this paragraph about? Write the sentence that contains the main idea.

Ice hockey is one of the fastest of all team sports.

_____

4. Now look for sentences with details that support the main idea. Write one sentence that contains details that describe the main idea more fully.

Its players race across the rink on ice skates.

_____

5. Hockey players are constantly on the move. Look at another detail in one of the sentences in the paragraph. How does it describe the main idea more fully? Write the detail and explain.

The game does not stop even when players

are substituted.

_____

COMPREHENSION

UNIT 2 Dollars and Sense • **Lesson 1** *Starting a Business*

▶ The /ə/ Sound

SPELLING

▶ The ə sound is the vowel sound in the unstressed syllable of a word.

▶ The stressed syllable of a word is the syllable that is pronounced stronger.

les•son   crim•son

▶ The first syllable of the words *lesson* and *crimson* is the stressed syllable. The /ə/ sound is the letter *o* in the last syllable of each word, because the last syllable is the unstressed syllable.

cus•tom	per•son	kit•ten	hap•pen	sea•son
but•ton	prob•lem	o•pin•ion	gar•den	mit•ten

 Pronunciation Strategy Write the words in which the /ə/ sound is spelled *e*.

1. gar•d<u>e</u>n
2. mit•t<u>e</u>n
3. hap•p<u>e</u>n
4. prob•l<u>e</u>m
5. kit•t<u>e</u>n

Write the words in which the /ə/ sound is spelled *o*.

6. sea•s<u>o</u>n
7. per•s<u>o</u>n
8. but•t<u>o</u>n
9. cus•t<u>o</u>m
10. o•pin•i<u>o</u>n

UNIT 2 Dollars and Sense • **Lesson 1** *Starting a Business*

▶ Suffixes *-ly* and *-ing*

Adding *-ly* to words creates adverbs, which describe the way something occurs. *(swiftly, expertly)*

If a word ends in *y*, the *y* is changed to *i* before adding *-ly*. *(lucky, luckily)*

The *-ing* ending shows that something is happening right now.

For words ending in *e*, drop the *e* before adding *-ing*. *(practice, practicing)*

For words ending in short vowel plus *p* or short vowel plus *t*, double the final consonant before adding *-ing*. *(nap, napping; hit, hitting)*

Practice Complete the math sentences.

1. analyze – e + ing = **analyzing**

2. brainstorm + ing = **brainstorming**

3. realistical + ly = **realistically**

4. merry – y + i + ly = **merrily**

5. tap + p + ing = **tapping**

VOCABULARY

▶Types of Sentences

GRAMMAR AND USAGE

Rule	Example
▶A **simple sentence** has one simple or compound subject and one simple or compound predicate.	▶Abraham Lincoln was a lawyer and was voted our 16th president.
▶Two independent clauses, simple sentences, joined with a comma and a coordinating conjunction form a **compound sentence**.	▶Eleven states left the Union, **but** the nation was eventually reunited.

Practice

▶Circle the simple subjects and underline the simple predicates in these sentences.

1. (Woodrow Wilson) and (Herbert Hoover) were two of our presidents.

2. (Veterinarians) give medicine to and operate on animals.

3. (Hawaii) and (Alaska) are the two states that are not connected to mainland United States.

4. (California) has a mild, sunny climate, and many (towns) there have become resorts.

▶Read the sentences. Write in the blank whether each one is a simple sentence or a compound sentence.

5. _simple_____ Eagles and hedgehogs are desert dwellers.

6. _compound_____ Red is a good color, but yellow is my favorite.

7. _simple_____ Every day, factories and homes use huge amounts of water.

Name _____ Date _____

▶Sentence Combining

Combining sentences is one way to improve sentences that are short and choppy. There are a number of ways to combine sentences.

▶ Combine two simple sentences by adding a conjunction to form a compound sentence.

Example

I missed the bus. Now I'll be late.   I missed the bus, and now I'll be late.

▶ Combine parts of sentences to form a new sentence with a compound subject or a compound predicate.

Example

Nora wrote about frogs. Stan wrote about frogs.   **Nora and Stan** wrote about frogs. (compound subject)

Nora sharpened her pencil. Nora began to write.   Nora **sharpened her pencil and began to write**. (compound predicate)

If your sentences are all short, or all of the same length, try combining some of them. Sentences of different lengths and styles are more interesting to read than sentences that are all the same.

Practice **Combine each of the following pairs of simple sentences. Write your new sentence in the space provided.** **Answers may vary. Possible answers are given.**

1. He walked around the park. I walked around the park.
   He and I walked around the park.

2. Monty jumped the fence. Monty ran down the block.
   Monty jumped the fence and ran down the block.

3. Heidi is in college. She is coming home this weekend.
   Heidi is in college, but she is coming home this weekend.

4. Jacob read that book. He liked it.
   Jacob read that book, and he liked it.

WRITER'S CRAFT

▶ The /ow/ and /oi/ Sounds

SPELLING

> The /ow/ sound is spelled *ou_* and *ow*.
>
> The /oi/ sound is spelled *oi* and *_oy*.
>
> In the final position, the /oi/ sound is always spelled *oy (enjoy)*.
>
> The spelling *oi* for the /oi/ sound is found in the beginning and/or middle of a word, but never at the end *(choice)*.

 Visualization Strategy Fill in the missing letters in the following words and rewrite the words on the lines provided.

1. gr_ _nd   =   **ground**

2. b_ _nd   =   **bound**

3. j_ _nt   =   **joint**

4. t_ _er   =   **tower**

5. cho_ce   =   **choice**

6. amo_nt   =   **amount**

7. mo_ntain   =   **mountain**

8. p_ _son   =   **poison**

9. empl_ _   =   **employ**

10. ab_ _ t   =   **about**

Antonyms

> **Antonyms** are words that are opposite or almost the opposite of another word.
>
> **front** and **back**   **left** and **right**

Practice

▶ **Use these words to complete the exercise below.**

young	slender	proper	hot	close
tall	rapid	dark	firm	poor

▶ **Complete the antonym pairs with a word from the box.**

1. slow   **rapid**
2. soft   **firm**
3. wrong   **proper**
4. old   **young**
5. fat   **slender**
6. rich   **poor**
7. cold   **hot**
8. light   **dark**
9. short   **tall**
10. open   **close**

VOCABULARY

▶Capitalization

GRAMMAR AND USAGE

Rule	Example
▶ Capitalize the first word in a sentence.	▶ In 1908, Henry Ford produced the Model T Ford car.
▶ Capitalize proper nouns, all important words in titles of works, and the names of months, days, and holidays.	▶ Mr. Alvarez Marshall Islands *The Velveteen Rabbit* July Monday Thanksgiving Day

Practice

▶**Rewrite the words below, using the correct capitalization.**

1. south dakota   **South Dakota**

2. saturday   **Saturday**

3. new year's day   **New Year's Day**

4. dr. miller   **Dr. Miller**

5. february   **February**

6. pacific ocean   **Pacific Ocean**

▶**Rewrite each title below, using the correct capitalization. Underline titles of works when handwritten.**

7. *little women* **Little Women**

8. *the adventures of huckleberry finn*
   The Adventures of Huckleberry Finn

9. *the sword in the stone* **The Sword in the Stone**

Organizing Expository Writing

Three common methods of organizing expository writing are compare and contrast, cause and effect, and question and answer.

You can **compare and contrast** two things to point out how they are alike and how they are different. This method works well for comparing two products or two characters in a book or movie, for example.

You can explore **causes and effects**. You might explain how several events caused another event. Or you might explain what causes mold to form on bread.

Or you can use a **question-and-answer approach**. Begin by asking a question. Then give the answer by explaining the process or providing background for the readers.

Practice For each topic, tell what the best method of organization would be—compare and contrast, cause and effect, or question and answer.

1. the change created by hiring a new school cook
   cause and effect or compare and contrast
   _____

2. why the class pet died
   question and answer or cause and effect
   _____

3. a book and a movie
   compare and contrast
   _____

WRITER'S CRAFT

▶ The /er/ Sound

SPELLING

> The /er/ sound is spelled *or, er, ear, ir,* and *ur.*
>
> The *ir* spelling for the /er/ sound is always in the middle of or at the end or a word.

Use these words to complete the exercise below.

worth	learn	serve	birth	early
shower	urge	thirst	heart	burst

Consonant Substitution Strategy Write the spelling word that is created by adding, dropping, or substituting one or more consonants in the following words.

1. earn   **learn**

2. yearly   **early**

3. first   **thirst**

4. forth   **worth**

5. durst   **burst**

6. mirth   **birth**

7. swerve   **serve**

8. hear   **heart**

9. tower   **shower**

10. purge   **urge**

UNIT 2 Dollars and Sense • **Lesson 3** *Elias Sifuentes, Restaurateur*

▶Shades of Meaning

Different words can have shades of meaning that relate to similar emotions or feelings. Most of the time these words are adjectives, such as *irritated*, *angry*, and *enraged*.

▶**Complete each sentence with a word from the box.**

hungry	famished	starving

1. I was __**hungry**__ because I skipped lunch.

2. I was __**famished**__ because I skipped lunch and dinner.

chilly	cold	frozen

3. During autumn the air is __**chilly**__.

4. During winter the air is __**cold**__.

5. The ice cubes were __**frozen**__.

VOCABULARY

▶ Periods and End Punctuation

GRAMMAR AND USAGE

Rule	Example
▶ Use a period at the end of a declarative sentence and most imperative sentences.	▶ We will attend the new play tonight. Come to dinner now, Amelia.
▶ Use periods with titles, street addresses, and some abbreviations.	▶ Ms. Albright 40 Main Ave. 4 oz.
▶ A question mark is used at the end of an interrogative sentence.	▶ What time is your English class?
▶ An exclamation point is used at the end of an exclamatory sentence.	▶ What an exciting touchdown!

Practice

▶ **Put periods where they are needed in these sentences.**

1. Sen.Smith is a member of the U.S.Congress.

2. Michigan Ave.is a famous street in Chicago.

3. Ms.Bailey, may I borrow a pencil, please?

4. Can you run 3 mi.in an hour?

▶ **Read the sentences and add the correct end punctuation to each.**

5. Have you heard of the United States Supreme Court**?**

6. It is the highest court in our country**.**

7. What an awesome responsibility that must be**!**

UNIT 2 Dollars and Sense • **Lesson 3** *Elias Sifuentes, Restaurateur*

▶ Dialogue and Direct Speech

When characters in a story talk, their conversation is called dialogue. When readers "hear" characters talk, it makes the characters seem more like real people. Good dialogue makes a story more interesting.

Dialogue is also a way to reveal details about characters. What a person says and how she says it tells readers what kind of person she is. Readers also learn about characters by hearing what *other* characters say about them.

When writing dialogue, keep these rules in mind:

▶ Each character's exact words are enclosed in quotation marks.

▶ A new paragraph begins each time the speaker changes.

▶ Punctuation for dialogue goes inside quotation marks.

▶ Speaker tags, such as *asked Mr. Hahn* and *he said*, must be used often enough for readers to keep track of who is speaking.

Practice Turn the following sentences into dialogue. Punctuate your dialogue correctly.
Answers will vary. Possible answers are given.

1. Barry asked his parents for five dollars. His mom asked why he needed money.

   "Mom? Dad? Could I please have five dollars?" asked

   Barry. "What do you need the money for?" his mom asked.

2. Emma thanked Aunt Linda for the sweater she gave her for her birthday. Aunt Linda said she hoped it fit well.

   "Thank you for the great birthday sweater, Aunt Linda,"

   said Emma.

   "Oh, I hope it fits well," replied her aunt.

▶Sequence

COMPREHENSION

Focus Sequence is the order in which things happen in a story. A writer uses time and order words to help the reader follow the sequence in a story.

Time and order words help a reader follow the sequence in a story.

- **Order words** show the order in which things take place. Words such as *first, then, next,* and *finally* show order.

- **Time words** show how time passes in a story. Words such as *spring, tomorrow,* and *morning* show time.

Practice

▶ Look at the pictures. Put the pictures in the proper sequence. Write the correct order word in the picture. Use the order words **first, then,** and **finally.**

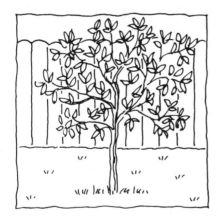

finally
_____

first
_____

then
_____

UNIT 2 Dollars and Sense • **Lesson 4** *Food from the 'Hood: A Garden of Hope*

▶**Sequence**

▶**Look at the following sentences about "Food from the 'Hood: A Garden of Hope." Put the sentences in the proper sequence. Write the correct order word in front of the sentence. Use the order words** *first*, *next*, **and** *finally*.

1. **First** _____, the students at Crenshaw High wanted to rebuild their neighborhood after the riots.

2. **Finally** _____, Food from the 'Hood became a successful neighborhood business run by the students.

3. **Next** _____, the students started a business selling vegetables grown in their own garden. **Answers will vary. Possible answers are shown.**

▶**Look at the following sentences. Complete each sentence by filling in a time word. Use the time words in the box below.**

today	soon	evening
winter	summer	tomorrow

1. Dinner is usually served in the **evening** _____.

2. I will wash clothes **today, tomorrow or soon** _____.

3. Very **soon** _____ it will be my birthday.

4. My grandparents go to Florida in the **winter** _____ and stay through March.

5. Last year, California was very hot all **summer** _____ long.

6. Since today is Monday, **tomorrow** _____ will be Tuesday.

Apply Write the last sentence of the following sequence. Use an order word in your sentence. **Answers will vary.**

First, Gus stood at home base, baseball bat in hand. Next, the pitcher threw the ball, and then Gus swung the bat.

COMPREHENSION

▶ The /âr/ and /ar/ Sounds

SPELLING

> The /âr/ sound is spelled *ar*, *are*, *air*, or *ear*.
>
> The /ar/ sound is spelled *ar*.

 Visualization Strategy Write the spelling of the /âr/ or /ar/ vowel sound in each of the given words. Some of the words do not contain the /âr/ or /ar/ sound. The first one is done for you.

Four-Letter Word	/âr/ or /ar/ Spelling	Spelling Word	/âr/ or /ar/ Spelling
1. wear	ear	beware	are
2. pair	air	comparison	ar
3. harp	ar	carpeting	ar
4. mare	are	nightmare	are
5. farm	ar	harmed	ar
6. marry	ar	library	ar
7. rate		narrate	ar
8. pear	ear	prepare	are
9. read		declare	are
10. deer		remembered	

The /âr/ and /ar/ Sounds • Reteach

Synonyms

> **Synonyms** are words that have similar meanings.
>
> Examples of synonyms: **fat** and **plump**
> **large** and **big**
> **begin** and **start**

Practice

▶ **Use these words to complete the exercise.**

certain	painting	fixing	job	commotion

▶ **Use the words in the box to write a synonym for each underlined word.**

1. My <u>occupation</u> is mailcarrier. <u>**job**</u>

2. I enjoy <u>restoring</u> broken things. <u>**fixing**</u>

3. There is a <u>mural</u> on the wall of my apartment. <u>**painting**</u>

4. I am <u>confident</u> I wrote the correct answer to the question.
<u>**certain**</u>

5. The dogs running through the crowd at the parade caused a
<u>disturbance</u>. <u>**commotion**</u>

VOCABULARY

Name _____ Date _____

▶Commas

MECHANICS

Rule	**Example**
▶ Use a comma to separate items in a series.	▶ James likes soccer, snowboarding, and lacrosse.
▶ Use a comma in addresses and dates.	▶ We live in Columbus, Ohio. Her birthday is July 10, 1984.
▶ Use a comma in direct address and with interjections and introductory phrases.	▶ Simon, please start your homework. Yes, I have seen that movie. After the play, let's get ice cream.

Practice   **Put commas where needed in these sentences.**

1. The National Baseball Hall of Fame and Museum is in Cooperstown, New York.

2. I enjoy watching the Chicago Cubs, the Atlanta Braves, and the Houston Astros.

3. Mars, Jupiter, and Pluto are three of the planets that are farther from the sun than Earth is.

4. Liz, please read aloud the paragraph about gravity.

5. At the exhibit, we learned that Pearl Harbor was bombed on December 7, 1941.

6. Oh, what a great painting!

▶ Compare and Contrast

Comparing and contrasting is one way to organize information in expository writing. It is sometimes useful to compare and contrast two items, such as two products, two events, two people, or two characters.

To **compare** means to tell how two or more things are alike. To **contrast** means to tell how two or more things are different.

WRITER'S CRAFT

Practice Look at the pairs of items listed below. Write in the spaces how the items are alike and how they are different. **Answers will vary. Possible answers are given.**

Items	Alike	Different
1. bird–mouse	Both are animals. Both make nests. Both have several young at once.	A bird has feathers. Birds can fly. A mouse has fur. Mice cannot fly.
2. sun–moon	Both are in the sky above Earth. Both shine.	The sun shines during day. The moon shines at night. The sun is a star; the moon is not.
3. orange juice– apple juice	Both are drinks. Both are healthful. Both come from fruit.	Orange juice comes from oranges. Apple juice comes from apples.

UNIT 2 Dollars and Sense • **Lesson 5** *Business is Looking Up*

► # Vowel Sounds in Two-Syllable Words

SPELLING

Each syllable of a word should contain one vowel sound.

j<u>oy</u>•f<u>ul</u>   pr<u>e</u>•d<u>i</u>ct   <u>ech</u>•<u>o</u>   <u>ex</u>•p<u>er</u>t

Use these words to complete the exercise below.

suggest	slender	comment	infect	cannot
tablet	product	within	credit	napkin

 Pronunciation Strategy Write the words with the /a/, /e/, /i/, /o/, and /u/ sounds in the first syllable. Underline the vowel sound in the first syllable.

/a/

1. t<u>a</u>blet

2. c<u>a</u>nnot

3. n<u>a</u>pkin

/e/

4. cr<u>e</u>dit

5. sl<u>e</u>nder

/i/

6. w<u>i</u>thin

7. <u>i</u>nfect

/o/

8. pr<u>o</u>duct

9. c<u>o</u>mment

/u/

10. s<u>u</u>ggest

Vowel Sounds in Two-Syllable Words • **Reteach**

Name _____ Date _____

▶Base Word Families

A **base word** is a word that can stand alone. Base word families consist of different words you can make from a base word.

Base Word	Base Word Family Members
Move	moveable, moved, mover, moving, unmoved

 Use the suffixes *-ed*, and *-ing*, to write two base word family members for each base word.

1. search   searched   searching

2. tempt   tempted   tempting

3. pair   paired   pairing

4. surf   surfed   surfing

5. coax   coaxed   coaxing

VOCABULARY

UNIT 2 Dollars and Sense • **Lesson 5** *Business is Looking Up*

▶ Quotation Marks and Underlining

MECHANICS

Rule	Example
▶ Use quotation marks around the exact words of a speaker and around the title of a poem or a short story.	▶ "Early to bed and early to rise makes a man healthy, wealthy, and wise," said Benjamin Franklin. The longest poem ever written is the Indian epic "Mahabharata."
▶ Underline the title of a book, a movie, or a work of art when handwritten.	▶ Have you seen the movie *The Lion King?*

Practice Look at the titles listed in the chart below. Correct each of the titles in the left column by writing the new title in the right column with the correct capitalization and punctuation—quotation marks and underlining.

lemonade stand (poem)	**"Lemonade Stand"**
still life with apples (painting)	**Still Life with Apples**
star wars (movie)	**Star Wars**
out of the dust (book)	**Out of the Dust**
water lilies (painting)	**Water Lilies**
the waste land (poem)	**"The Waste Land"**
the wright brothers (book)	**The Wright Brothers**

Write the next line of dialogue. Be sure to include quotation marks.

Answers will vary. Sample answer is given.

"Tell me about your best friend," the teacher said.

Idea: "He is good at soccer and laughs at my jokes."

Name _____ Date _____

▶ Developing Expository Writing

> Expository writing is writing that informs or explains. In some cases, a writer may be so familiar with a topic that no research is necessary. In many cases, however, a writer may need to conduct research before writing an expository piece.
>
> Once a writer chooses a topic and a main idea, she must decide how best to support that main idea. It's important to think about what kind of information a main idea needs for support. Will the paragraphs be full of facts and statistics? Of reasons? Or of examples? It's possible that a combination of these may be used to support a main idea.

Practice Read each paragraph. Tell whether the writer uses facts, reasons, or examples to support the main idea.

1. Our town's location is why we have mild temperatures. In winter, heavy snow sometimes falls on the mountains to the west. By the time the storm gets to our valley, though, there is usually little snow left. We may get only flurries, or we may get rain. The mountains act as a barrier for us.

   facts
   _____

2. An after-school tutoring program would help our school. Across town, at Brentwood School, students can meet with tutors for an hour after school. That school's test scores were better this year than last year.

   examples
   _____

3. The number of students eating hot lunches at school is increasing. The school cook takes credit for improving the menu this year. Many parents say that busy schedules prevent them from packing lunches for their children.

   reasons
   _____

WRITER'S CRAFT

▶Digraphs

A digraph is two letters that make one sound.

A vowel digraph combines two vowel sounds.

*lou*d   *shaw*l   *choice*

The spellings for some long-vowel sound patterns such as *ea* and *oa* are not vowel digraphs.

A consonant digraph combines two consonant sounds.

*sh*ame   *ch*alk   *th*ing

Visualization Strategy Add the correct vowel or consonant digraph to each word to create a spelling word. Rewrite the words on the lines provided.

1. ma _ _ ine   **machine**

2. exh _ _ st   **exhaust**

3. stret _ _   **stretch**

4. c _ _ ch   **couch**

5. _ _ eat   **wheat**

6. pit _ _   **pitch**

7. lea _ _ es   **leashes**

8. s _ _ ces   **sauces**

9. mer _ _ ant   **merchant**

10. rea _ _   **reach**

SPELLING

▶Review

Adding **-ly** to words creates adverbs that describe the way something occurs. *(swiftly, expertly)*

Adding **-ing** to words shows that something is happening right now. (moving)

Practice Write the base word for each base word family member.

1. elderly   **elder** _____

2. partly   **part** _____

3. strumming   **strum** _____

4. seizing   **seize** _____

5. charting   **chart** _____

VOCABULARY

▶ Colons, Semicolons, and Other Marks

GRAMMAR AND USAGE

Rule	**Example**
▶ Use a colon to show hours and minutes.	▶ 1:35 a.m.
▶ Use a semicolon between two independent clauses that do not have a coordinating conjunction.	▶ I studied hard; therefore, I did well on the test.
▶ Use a hyphen in fractions that are spelled out.	▶ Add one-half cup of sugar to the frosting.
▶ Use parentheses around words that add information to a sentence.	▶ Tim (John's brother) is on the soccer team.

Practice Add colons, semicolons, and hyphens to the paragraph below.

Ben started cooking at 11:30 a.m. His recipe for snickerdoodles calls for one-third cup of shortening. The cookies will rise;however, then they will settle. By the time that Ben cleaned up, it was 1:45 p.m.

Write a sentence about something you enjoy doing. Use parentheses around additional information that you believe is helpful to your reader.

Answers will vary.

Idea: Hawaii (our 50th state) is a place I enjoy visiting

because I love surfing.

_____

_____

▶Plot

> The series of events in a story is called the plot. A good story has a plot with a clear beginning, middle, and end.
>
> In the **beginning**, the problem is introduced.
>
> In the **middle**, the characters struggle with the problem and how to solve it.
>
> The point at which the characters begin to solve the problem is called the **climax**. The problem is solved at the end of the story.

 **Following is a mixed-up sequence of events from a story. Rewrite the three events in the order in which they would happen in the story.**

▶ Steve "the String" makes the school basketball team.

▶ Steve pulls down eight rebounds, allowing his team to win a close game.

▶ Steve feels that he needs to be the team's leading rebounder because he's the tallest one on the team.

1. **Steve "the String" makes the school basketball team.** _____

2. **Steve feels that he needs to be the team's leading rebounder because he's the tallest one on the team.**

3. **Steve pulls down eight rebounds, allowing his team to win a close game.**

WRITER'S CRAFT

UNIT 2 Dollars and Sense • **Lesson 7** *The Milkmaid and Her Pail*

▶Review

The /ow/ sound is spelled *ou_* or *ow*.

The /oi/ sound is spelled *oi* or *_oy*.

The /er/ sound is spelled *or, er, ear, ir,* and *ur*.

The /âr/ sound is spelled *ar, are, air,* or *ear*.

The /ar/ sound is spelled *ar*.

Visualization Strategy Use the letters in the words to create three- or four-letter words. **Answers will vary.**

1. tower   **tow** _____

2. plow   **low** _____

3. harvest   **hear** _____

4. customer   **cost** _____

5. outside   **out** _____

6. aware   **ear** _____

7. prepare   **pear** _____

8. joint   **not** _____

9. destroy   **does** _____

10. bound   **bun** _____

UNIT 2 Dollars and Sense • **Lesson 7** *The Milkmaid and Her Pail*

▶Review

> A **synonym** is a word that is similar in meaning to another word.
>
> *large* and *big*   *tardy* and *late*
>
> An **antonym** is a word that means the opposite, or almost the opposite, of another word.
>
> *front* and *back*   *left* and *right*

▶ **Use these words to complete the exercise below.**

rapid	firm	riot	vanished	confident

▶ **Write the vocabulary word that fits the synonyms and antonyms.**

Synonym	Antonym	
1. displaced	found	**vanished**
2. disturbance	peace	**riot**
3. certain	unsure	**confident**
4. quick	slow	**rapid**
5. hard	soft	**firm**

VOCABULARY

▶Review

Types of Sentences

▶ Circle the simple subjects and underline the simple predicates in these sentences.

1. (Sandro Botticelli) and (Hieronymus Bosch) <u>were</u> famous painters of the fifteenth century.

2. (Egypt) <u>is</u> a country in northeast Africa, and (Venezuela) <u>is</u> a country in northeast South America.

▶ **Capitalization/Periods and End Punctuation/Commas**

Rewrite these sentences with correct capitalization and punctuation.

3. the science experiment called for 5 oz hot water
   The science experiment called for 5 oz. hot water.

4. we plan to travel to seattle washington
   We plan to travel to Seattle, Washington.

5. their wedding is on january 4 2003
   Their wedding is on January 4, 2003.

Add quotation marks where needed in these sentences.

6. My favorite poem is "Ode to a Farmer."

7. Have you read the story "Barnyard Animals"?

Supporting Details

A good paragraph has two elements. First, it has a main idea, which is often stated in the first sentence of the paragraph. Then, the rest of the paragraph supports, or tells more about, the main idea. Those are the **supporting details**.

Different kinds of writing require different kinds of details. Supporting details might be reasons, examples, description, or facts.

The important thing about supporting details is that they tell more about the main idea of the paragraph. If they don't, they don't belong in that paragraph.

Practice **Look at the main ideas and details. Write an *X* next to the sentence that might support the main idea.**

1. Main idea: As a child, Amanda dreamed of studying dinosaurs.

_____ Her parents loved to read stories to her.

X_____ She had read every dinosaur book in the school library.

_____ Amanda had stars on the ceiling of her bedroom.

2. Main idea: Carmine is a stamp collector.

X_____ He has stamps from over 43 countries.

_____ On Tuesdays he has piano lessons.

_____ His favorite food is spaghetti.

3. Main idea: Moira's family owns a farm.

_____ She likes going to the art museum.

X_____ They sell vegetables at the farmer's market.

_____ Last week their car broke down.

WRITER'S CRAFT

UNIT 3 From Mystery to Medicine • **Lesson 1** *Medicine: Past and Present*

▶ The /j/ Sound and the /s/ Sound

SPELLING

> The /j/ sound can be spelled *g* before the letters *e* and *i*.
> *gentle*   *giraffe*
>
> The /s/ sound can be spelled *c* before the letters *e*, *i*, and *y*.
> *cell*   *cinnamon*   *cymbals*

Visualization Strategy
Circle the words with the /j/ sound spelled *ge* or *gi_* and the /s/ sound spelled *ce* or *ci_*. Rewrite the word on the line provided.

1. genius   **genius** _____

2. gone   _____

3. garden   _____

4. general   **general** _____

5. great   _____

6. contain   _____

7. certain   **certain** _____

8. charm   _____

9. citizen   **citizen** _____

10. century   **century** _____

▶Concept Words

> **Concept words** are specific words that help you understand and discuss a certain topic. For example, if you want to understand the ideas about medicine discussed in the selection "Medicine: Past and Present," you need to know the meanings of concept words like *epidemic*, *bacteria*, *vaccine*, *sterilize*, and *immune*.
>
> **epidemic:** an outbreak of a disease that spreads very quickly among many people in an area
>
> **bacteria:** tiny living cells that are microscopic; some cause disease
>
> **vaccine:** a liquid containing weakened germs of a disease that helps the body fight off the disease
>
> **sterilize:** to rid of bacteria
>
> **immune:** protected from a disease

VOCABULARY

Complete each sentence with a concept word in the box. Use the clues provided in the sentences to help you complete the exercise.

1. The Black Plague was an **epidemic** _____ in Europe, Asia, and Africa. Because there was no cure for The Black Plague, many people became ill.

2. A person who is **immune** _____ to a disease cannot become ill from that disease.

3. Some **bacteria** _____ cause diseases, but others do useful things, such as make soil richer.

4. The doctor used alcohol to **sterilize** _____, or rid his equipment of bacteria.

5. The first **vaccine** _____ was made from cowpox, a mild disease that people catch from cattle, and was later given to people to fight off the disease smallpox.

▶ Apostrophes

MECHANICS

Rule	**Example**
▶ In a contraction, an apostrophe takes the place of a letter or letters.	▶ I'll (I will)
▶ Use an apostrophe to show possession.	▶ it's (it is *or* it has)
	▶ Jenny's cup (the cup that belongs to Jenny)
	▶ girls' chairs (the chairs that belong to the girls)

Practice

▶ **Change the nouns on the left to show ownership of the things on the right. Write the possessive noun and the thing on the space provided.**

Owners	Things	Possessive
1. boy	glove	**boy's glove**
2. dogs	bones	**dogs' bones**
3. children	jackets	**children's jackets**

▶ **Make contractions from the words below.**

4. are not   **aren't**

5. we have   **we've**

▶ **Write a sentence using the contraction or possessive form of the following words:**

6. we are   **Answers will vary.**

7. the shoes that belong to Sam _____

▶ Avoiding Wordiness

When writing is wordy, readers may lose interest or get confused. Good writers use only as many words as they need. And they make every word count.

Here are some ways to avoid wordiness in your sentences.

▶ Remove groups of repetitive or unnecessary words.

▶ Replace complicated or very formal words with more simple ones.

▶ Shorten a clause to a phrase or even to a single word.

 **Rewrite each sentence, either removing unnecessary words or replacing wordy phrases with simpler ones.** **Answers may vary.**

1. The kite was floating so peacefully up there in the sky.

   The kite was floating so peacefully.

2. Ronnie likes colors that remind him of the southwestern part of the United States.

   Ronnie likes colors that remind him of the Southwest.

3. In light of the fact that I am the secretary, I better take notes.

   Because I am the secretary, I better take notes.

4. The movie seemed to ramble on and keep going forever.

   The movie seemed to ramble on forever.

5. The green, leafy branches closed behind me like a closing gate.

   The green, leafy branches closed behind me like a gate.

6. In the event that students are late, they will receive a tardy mark.

   If students are late, they will receive a tardy mark.

WRITER'S CRAFT

▶ Drawing Conclusions

COMPREHENSION

Focus Drawing conclusions helps readers get more information from a story.

Here is how you **draw conclusions:**

▶ Look for bits of information or details about a character or an event in a story. Use these details to make a statement or draw a conclusion about that character or event.

▶ Sometimes a conclusion is stated in the story. Sometimes it is not. However, a conclusion is always supported by details in the story.

Practice Look at the groups of sentences below. The sentences in the first column are details. The sentences in the second column are possible conclusions. One conclusion is correct, and one is incorrect. Put an *X* next to the sentence that could be the conclusion to the first pair of sentences. The first one is done for you.

Details

1. Carmen likes all kinds of cheese.

   Cheddar is a kind of cheese.

2. Rover is a dog.

   All dogs are animals.

3. Tasha plays the cello.

   People who play the cello are musicians.

4. Oranges are citrus fruit.

   Citrus fruit grows on trees.

Conclusions

__**X**__ Carmen likes cheddar.

_____ Carmen does not like cheddar.

_____ Rover is an elephant.

__**X**__ Rover is an animal.

__**X**__ Tasha is a musician.

_____ Tasha plays the flute.

__**X**__ Oranges grow on trees.

_____ Oranges grow on vines.

Name _____ Date _____

▶**Drawing Conclusions**

COMPREHENSION

Read the paragraph. Then answer the following.

Marta hung her favorite red jacket on the hook behind the closet door. Roberta, Marta's younger sister, liked the red jacket as much as Marta.

"May I wear your red jacket today?" Roberta asked.

"Not today," Marta replied, "I will need to wear it later this evening. I'm sorry."

Marta left the bedroom and went downstairs to finish her chores. Roberta pouted and folded her arms in front of her. Roberta was disappointed.

She said to herself, reaching for the jacket, "I just want to wear the jacket to the park for a couple of hours."

Several hours later, Marta returned to the bedroom to get her jacket. She gasped. Her favorite red jacket was covered with a fresh layer of mud!

Answers will vary. Possible answers are shown.

5. The sentences in this paragraph contain many details. One detail is that Roberta asks Marta for permission to wear Marta's jacket. Write two more details you find in this paragraph.

Detail: **Roberta was disappointed.**

Detail: **The jacket was covered with mud.**

6. Judging by the details in this paragraph, what can you conclude?

Roberta wore Marta's jacket to the park and got it covered

with mud.

 **Read the following statement, and draw a conclusion.**

All fish swim.
A trout is a type of fish.

Conclusion: **Trout swim.**

▶The /k/ Sound

SPELLING

> The /k/ sound can be spelled *k*, *c*, or *_ck*.
>
> The *ck* spelling for the /k/ sound usually occurs in the middle or at the end or a word (*smack*).
>
> The /k/ sound is usually spelled *c* after the *i* sound at the end of a two-syllable word (*frantic*).

▶**Use these words to complete the exercise below.**

tracks	cart	check	rocket	nickel
attic	calm	bucket	lucky	picket

 Rhyming Strategy
Write the spelling words that rhyme with these words.

1. balm   **calm**

2. ticket   **picket**

3. socket   **rocket**

4. dart   **cart**

5. racks   **tracks**

6. deck   **check**

7. tucket   **bucket**

8. mucky   **lucky**

9. static   **attic**

10. pickle   **nickel**

▶Idioms

An **idiom** is a phrase or expression that has a different meaning than the literal meaning of its words. An idiom is often well known, like an old saying. For example, you may have heard the idiom "Her head was in the clouds." This statement is not meant to be taken literally and does not mean that her head is actually in the sky. It means that she is not paying attention.

Another expression of an idiom is "Peter kept his nose in a book all day." This statement does not mean that Peter's nose was actually stuck between the pages. It means that he was reading all day.

Circle the words or phrases that cause the sentences to be idioms.

1. Gloria and Camille (don't see eye to eye) on everything.

2. Matt (stole the spotlight.)

3. Alicia (drove a hard bargain.)

4. Christopher was (fishing for) the answer.

5. I'd (give my right arm to own a plane.)

VOCABULARY

Name _____ Date _____

▶ Verb Tenses

Rule	Example
▶ A verb shows an action or tells what someone or something is, was, or will be. To form the present tense of a regular verb, add *s* or *es*. To form the past tense, add *ed*. To form the future tense, add *will* to the verb.	▶ plays—played—will play ▶ uses—used—will use ▶ wishes—wished—will wish

Practice Choose a verb from the box and write it in the space to complete each sentence. Write in the blank at the end of each sentence whether the verb is present, past, or future tense.

will enjoy	increased	will visit	discovered	produces

1. People **discovered** _____ oil in Texas in 1901. **past** _____

2. You **will enjoy** _____ your hiking trip through the Sierra Nevada mountains next summer. **future** _____

3. Our uncle's factory in Kentucky **produces** _____ metals and machinery. **present** _____

▶ Think of an action scene, such as a ball game or a trip to a crowded, noisy mall. List verbs that will bring the scene to life. Then, write a paragraph using the verbs. Use a separate sheet of paper if you need more space.

Verbs: _____ **Answers will vary.** _____

Paragraph: _____

_____

Name _____ Date _____

 # Place and Location Words

> **Place and location words** help readers understand where things are or where actions take place. Here are some common place and location words:
>
> | | | | | | |
> |---|---|---|---|---|---|
> | about | above | across | along | among | around |
> | at | behind | beside | by | down | in, inside, into |
> | near | on | out, outside | over | past | through |
> | to | under | up | | | |
>
> In stories, writers use place and location words to help readers understand where characters are and what is happening.
>
> **Example**
>
> Mrs. Mason ran her finger <u>down</u> the recipe card. Yes, she had everything she needed. She got <u>down</u> the flour and sugar. She got butter and two eggs <u>out</u> of the fridge. One by one, she put things <u>into</u> her big mixing bowl. Mrs. Mason hummed as she stirred the dough <u>inside</u> the bowl.

Practice Write the place or location word you see in each sentence.

1. Across from me sat a man in a very tall hat.　**across**

2. We dashed outside for recess.　**outside**

3. During the parade, we ran behind the band.　**behind**

4. Inside my mittens, my fingers felt like ice.　**inside**

5. Kelsey lives one floor above me.　**above**

6. Taylor leaned against the fence.　**against**

7. Along the road were millions of wildflowers.　**along**

8. Fog settled in the valleys.　**in**

WRITER'S CRAFT

► Author's Point of View

COMPREHENSION

Focus Every story is told from a specific point of view. An author chooses the point of view from which a story is told.

In writing a story, the author creates a narrator, the person who tells the story from a particular point of view.

► In a story told from the **third-person point of view**, the narrator is an outside observer of the happenings in a story. The narrator uses pronouns such as *he, she,* and *they* when telling the story.

► In a story told from the **first-person point of view**, the narrator is a character in the story and uses pronouns such as *I, me,* and *my* when telling the story.

Practice Look at the sentences below. In the spaces provided, write the point of view of each sentence. Remember, first-person point of view uses pronouns such as *I, me,* and *my.* The third-person point of view uses pronouns such as *he, she,* and *they.*

1. They belong to the Girl Scouts. **third-person**

2. She does not know Callie. **third-person**

3. I am my brother's keeper. **first-person**

4. He is a talented artist. **third-person**

5. Valerie treated the wound on my arm. **first-person**

6. Helen gave the towel to me. **first-person**

7. I love the way Cara dances! **first-person**

8. She traveled to Italy last summer. **third-person**

Name _____ Date _____

▶ **Author's Point of View**

▶ Fill in the sentences below, using pronouns that show the first-person point of view. Use the pronouns *I, me,* and *my*.

9. __I_____ am nine years old.

10. __My_____ mother is a teacher at the high school.

11. __My_____ books are on the table.

12. This is all the money you gave __me_____.

▶ Fill in the sentences below using pronouns that show the third-person point of view. Use the pronouns *he, she,* and *they*.

13. __She_____ is the mother of three children.

14. Are __they_____ going to the carnival?

15. __He_____ is Cheryl's uncle.

16. Is __she or he_____ a doctor?

▶ Read the paragraph below. Then answer the questions.

My name is Craig, and I am an artist. I draw illustrations for the local newspaper. I have also drawn pictures for news magazines. On my own time, I paint pictures of birds.

What is the point of view of this paragraph? __first-person_____

Write the words that tell the point of view. __I, my_____

 Rewrite the following sentence using the third-person point of view.

My name is Craig, and I am an artist.

His name is Craig, and he is an artist.
_____

_____

COMPREHENSION

UNIT 3   From Mystery to Medicine • **Lesson 3** *The Bridge Dancers*

▶ The /j/ Sound

SPELLING

The /j/ sound can be spelled *ge* and *_dge*. The *_dge* spelling usually follows a short-vowel sound, as in *fudge*.

▶ **Use these words to complete the exercise below.**

badge	wedge	image	garbage	sausage
bridge	voyage	lodge	manage	judge

Visualization Strategy
Complete the spelling words by adding the letters *ge* or *dge*.

1. ima **ge** _____

2. we **dge** _____

3. ba **dge** _____

4. ju **dge** _____

5. voya **ge** _____

6. bri **dge** _____

7. garba **ge** _____

8. sausa **ge** _____

9. mana **ge** _____

10. lo **dge** _____

Metaphors

> A **metaphor** is an original comparison between two things that are not normally compared. A metaphor says that one thing **is** another thing, rather than saying it is **like** another thing. Here are some examples of metaphors:
>
> Peter is a clown.
> Roger's heart is an ice cube.
> We urged Rosa to finish her work, but she was a snail.
>
> These metaphors compare Peter to a clown, a heart to an ice cube, and Rosa to a snail. These comparisons are new and creative, and tell us something important about Peter, Roger's heart, and Rosa. Peter is funny, Roger is not loving, and Rosa works slowly.

Rewrite the sentences, making them metaphors. The first one is done for you. Answers may vary. Possible answers are shown.

1. John is very smart. John is a talking encyclopedia.

2. My room is as cold as ice. **My room was an icebox last night.**

3. **Every day I have to climb a mountain of homework.**

   I had a lot of homework last night.

4. Sunday was a snowy day. **A blanket of snow covered the farm.**

5. **Her heart is a fountain of kindness.** She is a very kind person.

VOCABULARY

UNIT 3 From Mystery to Medicine • **Lesson 3** *The Bridge Dancers*

▶ Subject-Verb Agreement

Rule	Example
▶ A singular subject has a verb that agrees in number. ▶ A plural subject has a verb that agrees in number.	▶ Paul walks. ▶ Joan runs. ▶ The senators applaud. ▶ The children stand.

Practice In the blanks below, write the verb in parentheses that correctly completes each sentence.

1. Wynton Marsalis (play, plays) **plays** _____ the trumpet.

2. His father and brothers (was, were) **were** _____ all jazz musicians.

3. Three states (border, borders) **border** _____ the Pacific Ocean.

▶ Complete each sentence with a verb that makes sense. Make sure the subject and the verb agree in number.

Answers will vary. Possible answers are shown.

4. Boris Becker and Pete Sampras **play** _____ tennis.

5. Weathering **changes** _____ the surface of Earth.

6. Annie Oakley **was** _____ a member of Buffalo Bill's Wild West Show.

▶ Think of a person whom you admire. Write a paragraph about some of the things you admire about this person. Make sure the subject and verb in each of your sentences agree in number. Use a separate sheet of paper if you need more space.

Answers will vary.

_____

_____

_____

Name _____ Date _____

► Figurative Language

Figurative language, or figures of speech, are words that stand for more than their literal meanings. Writers use figurative language to help create pictures in readers' minds.

Rule	**Example**
► A **simile** compares two things that are not alike by using the word *like* or *as*. In a simile, one thing is said to be *like* another.	► The lake looked like a mirror.
► A **metaphor** also compares two things that are not alike. A metaphor does not use *like* or *as*. In a metaphor, one thing is said to *be* another.	► The lake was a mirror.
► **Personification** is giving human qualities to objects or to plants or animals.	► Mopsy lay on the floor, thinking hard about where the mouse might be.
► **Exaggeration** is a writer's way of stretching the truth to add humor.	► Their house was so big that they could go for days without seeing each other.

WRITER'S CRAFT

Practice Tell whether each of the following sentences is an example of simile, metaphor, personification, or exaggeration.

1. **exaggeration** His arms were so long he could touch the ceiling and the floor at the same time.

2. **simile** The coffee was as black as tar.

3. **simile** The circus people swung up high like monkeys.

4. **personification** That last storm took our tallest, proudest pine tree.

5. **metaphor** The crow's cry was a warning that something was wrong.

▶ Fact and Opinion

Focus Writers use facts and opinions to support ideas in their writing.

> ▶ A **fact** is a statement that can be proven true.
>   A square has four sides. (You can prove this statement by drawing a square and counting the sides.)
>
> ▶ An **opinion** is what someone feels or believes is true.
>   An opinion cannot be proven true or false.
>   Blue squares are the best. (This statement cannot be proven true or false. It is a statement about what someone believes.)

Practice Read the following sentences. Ask yourself the question, "Can this sentence be proven true?" If it can be proven true, then it is a fact. Write an *X* next to each sentence that is a fact.

1. __X__ A triangle has three sides.

2. _____ The moon is made of cheese.

3. __X__ Cats have paws.

4. __X__ A bicycle has two wheels.

5. _____ All children are noisy.

6. __X__ The Amazon River is in South America.

7. _____ Basketball players are more talented than other athletes.

8. __X__ The surface of the sun is very hot.

9. __X__ The colors of the United States flag are red, white, and blue.

10. _____ Books are better than magazines.

COMPREHENSION

Name _____ Date _____

▶ **Fact and Opinion**

▶ **Read the following sentences. Ask yourself the question, "Can this sentence be proven true or false?" If it cannot be proven true or false, then it is an opinion. Write an *O* next to each sentence that is an opinion.**

11. _____ Lemons are yellow.

12. ___O___ Shoes are better than sandals.

13. ___O___ My birthday is the best day of the year.

14. _____ The English language has 26 letters in its alphabet.

15. _____ Orange juice contains vitamin C.

16. ___O___ Vanilla is the best flavor of ice cream.

17. _____ A chicken is a type of bird that does not fly.

18. ___O___ Mary is prettier than Carol.

19. _____ Astronauts have walked on the moon.

20. ___O___ My computer is better than Kit's.

▶ **Read the paragraph below. The paragraph has both facts and opinions. Draw one line under the facts. Draw two lines under the opinions.**

   I think aluminum cans are better than plastic bottles. Aluminum is one of the most common elements on this planet. This element makes up about 8 percent of Earth's crust. I believe aluminum cans are better because they come from the planet.

 **What's your opinion on recycling aluminum cans? Write a sentence stating your opinion.** **Answers will vary.**

_____

_____

COMPREHENSION

▶The /s/ Sound

The /s/ sound can be spelled *s*, *c*, *ce*, or *ss*.
same   *cent*   *cite*   *less*

▶**Use these words to complete the exercise below.**

spice	prance	twice	surface	brace
device	process	sentence	advice	chance

SPELLING

Visualization Strategy
Write the spelling words that are related to the words below.

1. bracing   **brace**

2. devised   **device**

3. spicy   **spice**

4. pranced   **prance**

5. chances   **chance**

6. surfacing   **surface**

7. two   **twice**

8. advised   **advice**

9. sentenced   **sentence**

10. processing   **process**

▶ Science Words

> **Science words** are concept words that are used to discuss and write about a variety of sciences. A scientist who studies plants may need to use science words such as *chlorophyll* and *stamen*, while a scientist who studies the stars may need to use words such as *dwarf* and *nebula*. Science words may seem difficult to define, but context clues can help.

▶ **Use these words to complete the exercise below.**

spider	moon	mammals	rain	ants
trees	mosquito	satellite	snow	flowers
spacecraft	sunshine	birds	cats	roots

▶ **Use the words in the box to write three concept words for each science topic.**

1. entomology–the study of insects

   ants   **spider**   **mosquito**

2. astronomy–the study of planets, stars, and heavenly bodies

   satellite   **spacecraft**   **moon**

3. meterology–the study of weather

   snow   **rain**   **sunshine**

4. zoology–the study of animals

   cats   **mammals**   **birds**

5. botany–the study of plants.

   flowers   **trees**   **roots**

VOCABULARY

► Pronoun-Antecedent Agreement

GRAMMAR AND USAGE

Rule	**Example**
► The noun to which a pronoun refers to in a sentence is called the **antecedent**. The pronoun must agree with its antecedent in number. ► A pronoun may replace a compound subject.	► **Benjamin Franklin** is famous for his almanac. **He** was also a statesman and a scientist. ► Friedtjof Nansen studied the Lapp **people** to see how **they** lived in polar conditions. ► **Alain Prost and Jeanne Longo** are well-known athletes. **They** are both from France.

Practice   Read the sentences. Replace each underlined pronoun with the correct pronoun. Write the correct pronoun above the underlined word.

him
1. Robert Schumann's music made <u>it</u> a leader of the Romantic movement in music.

They
2. Schumann wrote many pieces of music. <u>It</u> include two sonatas.

it
3. Because Asia is so big, <u>he</u> is a land of variety: high mountains, long rivers, and hot and cold climates.

They
4. Instincts are behaviors with which we are born. <u>It</u> are inherited from our parents.

► Write a sentence about a sport or sports that you like using a pronoun and a noun. Be sure that the pronoun and its antecedent agree in number. Answers will vary.

_____

_____

Name _____ Date _____

▶ Tone of a Personal Letter

The tone of a piece of writing is the feeling the writer conveys. A writer's tone may be serious, funny, or sad. A writer's tone is affected by the words he chooses and how he expresses himself.

In a personal letter, the tone should be friendly. It's not a business letter, after all. A good way to think of a personal letter is a one-way conversation with a friend. The writing may sound a lot like a conversation you would have with a classmate, a brother, or a sister.

In informal writing, such as a writer would use in a personal letter, the sentences may be short, like the ones we use in everyday conversation. Sentences may include contractions, abbreviations, and perhaps even slang. In general, the words are simple, not complicated.

Practice **Make an X in front of the five sentences that have a more friendly tone and that would be good to use in a personal letter. Remember that the sentences in a personal letter should sound like what you might say to a friend or sister or brother.**

1. _____ You must pardon me for not writing sooner.

2. __X__ My cousin and I went for a swim today.

3. __X__ Kelly's doing really well in first grade.

4. _____ I hope that you had a most pleasant trip to Atlanta.

5. __X__ My teacher thinks I should try out for the school play.

6. _____ I cannot bear this weather any more!

7. __X__ We're studying ocean life right now.

8. _____ Tico and I had a pleasant weekend together.

9. _____ I shall never be able to thank you for taking me to the concert.

10. __X__ I hope Uncle Max is feeling better.

► Making Inferences

COMPREHENSION

Focus Making inferences helps a reader understand the total picture in a story.

An **inference** is a statement you make when you read about a character or event in a story.

Here is what you use to make an inference.

► First, use **information** from the story. Facts and descriptions in a story are types of information you can use to make an inference.

► Combine the information from the story with your **personal experience** or knowledge to make an inference.

Practice Read the paragraph below. Then answer the questions on this page and the next.

Answers will vary. Possible answers are shown.

When Brian awoke, he did not remember much about what had happened in the operating room. He remembered the nurse holding a mask over his nose and mouth and telling him to breathe deeply. He remembered feeling very drowsy. Then everything and everybody in the room disappeared. Now, here he was back in his hospital room. His throat was very sore, but he felt fine. He wondered what actually had happened during the operation.

Brian asked the nurse, "Did Dr. Bryant really take out my tonsils?"

A fact is information you can use to make an inference. In the paragraph above, one fact is that Brian becomes drowsy in the operating room. Write another fact about the paragraph.

He remembered feeling very drowsy.

UNIT 3 From Mystery to Medicine • **Lesson 5** *The New Doctor*

 **Making Inferences**

COMPREHENSION

What do you know? Maybe you know what a sore throat feels like. Write something else you know that is related to the character or events in the paragraph.

Students may know something about procedures in a

hospital.

Read the following paragraphs. Think about the information and your knowledge about the characters and events in each paragraph. Then, complete each inference below with the correct word.

Madeline's job was to blow up as many balloons as possible. Josh helped hang blue and white streamers in the dining room. Since Dad was the tallest, he hung the big "Happy Birthday" sign over the doorway. Madeline said, "Casey will be very surprised when he comes home!"

Inference: Who is celebrating a birthday? **Casey**

"Don't forget the sunscreen," Mom said. I grabbed the sunscreen from the medicine cabinet and put it in the bag with the rest of the stuff. I said to myself, "Let's see . . . we have three beach towels, an umbrella, and rubber sandals. Oh! I must bring my bucket and shovel. I want to build an enormous sand castle today."

Inference: Where is the family going? **to the beach**

 **Make another inference from the paragraph above. Write your statement here.**

Answers will vary. Possible answers are shown.

The narrator likes building sand castles.

_____

UNIT 3 From Mystery to Medicine • **Lesson 5** *The New Doctor*

▶ The /ch/ Sound

SPELLING

> The /ch/ sound is spelled *ch* at the beginning of a word.
>
> The /ch/ sound is often spelled *tch* at the end of a word after a short vowel, as in *latch*.

▶ **Use these words to complete the exercise below.**

torch	reach	wrench	starch	branch
fetch	watch	twitch	chatter	pinch

Consonant Substitution Strategy
Write the spelling words that are created by adding, dropping, or substituting one or more consonants.

1. patch   **watch**

2. retch   **fetch**

3. ranch   **branch**

4. scatter   **chatter**

5. teach   **reach**

6. porch   **torch**

7. cinch   **pinch**

8. trench   **wrench**

9. parch   **starch**

10. pitch   **twitch**

▶Spanish Words

As you read stories like the one told in the selection "The New Doctor," you may come across words from different languages such as Spanish. These words help make the story more realistic by showing how the characters actually speak. You may not know the meanings of these words unless you speak that language yourself. But you can try to figure out the meaning from context clues.

Before you can discover the meanings of Spanish words, you must learn to recognize them in the texts you read. Spanish words frequently end with the vowels *a* or *o*.

Read the following sentences, and complete the definitions beneath with a Spanish word. The sentences should give you a clue to the meaning of each word.

There were people dancing during the **fiesta.**
There was meat in the **tortilla.**
My **amigos** and I play football together.
It was impossible for me to climb the **mesa**; it was too high.
The **curandera** taught my mother how to use herbs to heal a wound.

1. a party ___fiesta___

2. a healer who uses remedies such as herbs ___curandera___

3. a thin, round, flat bread made with flour ___tortilla___

4. friends ___amigos___

5. a hill or mountain with a flat top and steep sides ___mesa___

VOCABULARY

▶ Intensive, Reflexive, and Demonstrative Pronouns

GRAMMAR AND USAGE

Rule	Example
▶ An **intensive pronoun** draws attention to another noun or pronoun in the same sentence.	▶ He **himself** gave the speech to Congress.
▶ A **reflexive pronoun** refers to the subject of the sentence as the thing or person receiving the action.	▶ We imagined **ourselves** on the hayride.
▶ A **demonstrative pronoun** points out a specific person, place, or thing.	▶ **this** chair (nearby) ▶ **those** books (far away)

Practice

▶ **Fill in the blank with an intensive or reflexive pronoun.**

1. When spies send messages, the spies **themselves** write them in code to hide their meaning.

2. Mozart wrote 30 symphonies **himself**.

3. I timed **myself** on my mile run.

4. They **themselves** are responsible for the program.

5. The snake **itself** can get its prey in the wild.

6. She taught **herself** the states and their capitals.

▶ **Write a sentence using a demonstrative pronoun describing something far away.**

Idea: I saw a giant tortoise in that habitat on the other

side of the zoo.

Aim, Purpose, and Audience

> A writer's **aim** is the message he or she wants to convey. The aim is closely tied to the writer's purpose for writing. For example, the aim of a writer who publishes an informative article about pet geckos might be simply to share her knowledge. Her aim may also be to raise readers' awareness of the care such animals require. So she is doing more than just *informing* her readers, even though that is her basic purpose for writing.
>
> A writer's **purpose** may be to inform, to explain, to entertain, or to persuade. In some cases, a writer may have more than one purpose.
>
> The **audience** is the people who will read or hear the written product. It's important to know who the audience is as you write. For example, if you are writing for your teacher, you may use different words or a different tone than if you are writing for your best friend.

Practice Read each writing topic below. Tell whether the writer's purpose is to inform, to explain, to entertain, or to persuade.

1. **persuade** _____ why the speed limit should be lower

2. **explain** _____ the difference between gold and fool's gold

3. **inform** _____ cliff dwellers of the Southwest

4. **entertain** _____ nine reasons to get out of bed *before* you brush your teeth

Tell what kind of audience each of these products might be written for. Be as specific as you can. **Answers will vary. Possible answers are given.**

5. a report about the English civil war

   a teacher; people interested in the English civil war

6. a magazine article about raising toddlers

   parents; preschool teachers

WRITER'S CRAFT

► Cause and Effect

COMPREHENSION

Focus Cause-and-effect relationships help readers understand why events happen in a certain way.

> ► A **cause** is why something happens.
>
> ► The **effect** is what happens as a result.
>
> | Cause | | Effect |
> |---|---|---|
> | The drummer hits the drum with her stick. | ⟶ | The drum makes a sound. |
>
> Writers sometimes use signal words to show cause-and-effect relationships. Signal words, such as *because*, *so*, *if*, *then*, and *since*, help readers know what happens and why it happens.

Practice Match each cause with its effect by drawing a line.

1. Runners race around the track.

2. The small hand goes around the clock.

3. The boy falls in the lake.

4. An artist places paint on a canvas.

5. The fish moves its tail.

6. Water is placed in ice-cube trays in the freezer.

7. Yellow and red paint are blended.

8. Water is placed on a sidewalk on a hot day.

a. An hour passes.

b. The boy gets wet.

c. The fish swims.

d. One of the racers wins the race.

e. Orange paint is made.

f. A picture is made.

g. The water freezes.

h. The water evaporates.

▶ **Cause and Effect**

Look at the following sentences. Some of the sentences show a cause-and-effect relationship. Others do not. Draw an *X* next to the sentences that show a cause-and-effect relationship. Look for signal words such as *because, if, then,* and *so*. Underline the signal words in the sentences that show cause and effect.

9. __X__ <u>Because</u> I was going too fast, I got a speeding ticket.

10. _____ A mouse and an elephant are both animals.

11. _____ We went to the movies and then to the pet shop.

12. __X__ <u>If</u> I babysit my little brother, <u>then</u> I get paid.

13. __X__ My grandfather is old, <u>so</u> he must have experienced a lot.

14. _____ The team is playing at the stadium, which is the largest place in town.

15. __X__ Liz's coat is on the chair, <u>so</u> she must be here.

16. __X__ I hear the bell, <u>so</u> class must be starting.

17. _____ The sewing machine is new and has all the latest features.

18. __X__ <u>Because</u> it is snowing, I will wear my boots.

19. _____ Snowboarding is difficult but very fun.

20. __X__ <u>If</u> the cake is missing, <u>then</u> the dog must have eaten it.

 **Write an effect for the following cause.**

Answers will vary.

Because we had a vacation from school today, _____

_____

The Story of Susan La Flesche

UNIT 3 **From Mystery to Medicine • Lesson 6** *Picotte*

▶ The /sh/ Sound

SPELLING

The /sh/ sound is spelled *sh, _ci_,* or *_ti_.* The /sh/ sound can be spelled *_ci_* when followed by the endings **-ous, -al, -an,** or **-ent.** The /sh/ sound can be spelled *_ti_* in the ending **-tion** and before the ending **-ous.**

Use these words to complete the exercise below.

publish	official	shatter	direction	ancient
special	vicious	social	delicious	instruction

Visualization Strategy
Circle the correct spelling for each word. Write the correct spelling on the lines provided.

1. anshent	(ancient)	antient	**ancient**
2. publeash	(publish)	publishe	**publish**
3. (social)	sotial	soshal	**social**
4. (official)	offitial	offishal	**official**
5. instrucshon	instruccion	(instruction)	**instruction**
6. delictious	(delicious)	delishious	**delicious**
7. (direction)	direcshon	direcion	**direction**
8. shartter	chartter	(shatter)	**shatter**
9. speshal	(special)	spetial	**special**
10. vitious	vishious	(vicious)	**vicious**

The /sh/ Sound • Reteach

▶Concept Words

You will remember that **concept words** are words that are used to write about or understand a certain subject. The selection "The Story of Susan La Flesche Picotte" contains a number of concept words used to describe the experience of Susan La Flesche Picotte, the first female Native American doctor in the United States.

Use these words to complete the exercise below.
inundated–covered with a flood or overwhelmed.
siege–a persistent attack.
grippe–a contagious flu-like disease.
pneumonia–a disease of the lungs that causes trouble breathing.
snowstorm–a storm with strong winds and much snow.

Complete each sentence with a word from the box.

1. After my cousin became ill with **grippe** _____ we were told to stay away from her because she was contagious.

2. A person who has **pneumonia** _____ might cough or have a hard time breathing.

3. Because it rained for three days, the town became **inundated** _____ with water.

4. The **snowstorm** _____ signaled the beginning of winter.

5. The herd of lions surrounded the antelopes in a **siege** _____ of the mother and her calf.

VOCABULARY

▶ Adjectives and Adverbs

Rule	Example
▶ An **adjective** is a word that tells *what kind*, *which one*, and *how many*.	▶ **blue** sweater ▶ **loud** music ▶ **fluffy** sweater ▶ **smelly** fish ▶ President Lincoln spoke **movingly.** (describes *spoke*)
▶ **Adverbs** describe verbs, adjectives, and other adverbs.	▶ Mica feels **very** smooth. (describes *smooth*) ▶ We don't go there **too** often. (describes *often*)

Practice　Look at the sentences below. Underline the adjectives once. Underline the noun or pronoun that the adjective describes twice.

1. Roosevelt had a good plan for our country.

2. Margot Fonteyn was a famous ballerina.

3. Woodlands can be moist and shady.

▶ **Look at the sentences below. Draw one line under the adverb. Draw two lines under the verb that the adverb describes.**

4. A peninsula is a body of land that is almost surrounded by water.

5. The North American pitcher plant slowly digests insects that it has trapped.

6. The principal visits our classroom often.

▶ **Rewrite the following sentence using adjectives and adverbs to make the sentence more interesting and descriptive.**

The senator spoke.

Answers will vary.

_____

Time and Order Words

When writers tell about steps or events that happen in a certain order, they use time and order words to tell when things happen and in what order they happen.

Time words and phrases tell when things happen.

today	after class	in the morning	next week
Friday	one month	last summer	a year ago

Order words tell in what order events happen.

after	before	finally	first	last	later
meanwhile	next	second	then	third	until

Notice how the time and order words in this paragraph make the instructions clear.

Example

   And <u>now</u> I'll let you in on a secret recipe. <u>First</u>, make one piece of toast. Spread peanut butter on the toast. <u>Next</u>, slice half a banana. Lay the slices flat to cover the peanut butter. <u>Then</u> lay two strips of bacon on top of the bananas. <u>Finally</u>, take a bite and enjoy.

WRITER'S CRAFT

Practice Read each sentence or passage. Then write the time and order words and phrases you find in each passage.

1. My cast comes off in a month.

   month

2. George has answered my e-mail at last.

   at last

3. I'll call before the next meeting.

   before

4. My sister and I meet at noon to share our lunch.

   at noon

5. Last week I watched a show about Sarah Chang.

   Last week

6. Cal waited for an hour in the dentist's office.

   an hour

7. I gave up on the bus, then hiked to the park.

   then

UNIT 3 From Mystery to Medicine • **Lesson 7** *Shadow of a Bull*

SPELLING

►Review

The /j/ sound can be spelled *g* before the letters *e* and *i*.
The /j/ sound can also be spelled *ge* and *dge* at the end of a word.
The /s/ sound can be spelled *c* before the letters *e*, *i*, and *y*.
The /s/ sound can also be spelled *s*, *ce*, or *ss*.
The /k/ sound can be spelled *k*, *c*, or *_ck*.
The /ch/ sound can be spelled *ch* and *_tch*.

► **Use these words to complete the exercise below.**

| touching | advice | watch | nickel | image |
| century | fancy | judge | general | gently |

Visualization Strategy
Fill in the missing sounds and rewrite the words
correctly on the lines provided.

1. _ entury — **century**

2. ni _ _ el — **nickel**

3. wa _ _ _ — **watch**

4. _ _ neral — **general**

5. advi _ _ — **advice**

6. tou _ _ ing — **touching**

7. _ ently — **gently**

8. fan _ _ — **fancy**

9. ju _ _ _ — **judge**

10. ima _ _ — **image**

Name _____ Date _____

▶ Metaphors

As you learned earlier in this unit, a **metaphor** is an original comparison between two things that are not normally compared. A metaphor says that one thing **is** another thing, rather than saying it is **like** another thing.

Example: His stomach is a bottomless pit.
The clouds were fluffy clumps of cotton candy.

Read the following sentences and answer the questions beneath them.

1. The track star ran faster than a streak of lightning.
   What two things are being compared?

   running fast and streak of lightning

2. Her curly eyebrows were wriggling, woolly caterpillars.
   What two things are being compared?

   curly eyebrows and wriggling, woolly caterpillars

3. His new car turned out to be a real lemon.
   What two things are being compared?

   new car and lemon

4. The tree's shadow was a giant spider on the bedroom wall.
   What two things are being compared?

   the tree's shadow and a giant spider

5. The frozen pond is a smooth, chilly tabletop.
   What two things are being compared?

   frozen pond and smooth, chilly tabletop.

VOCABULARY

▶Review

GRAMMAR AND USAGE

Practice Write the words that form the contractions below.

▶ **Apostrophes**

1. wouldn't ___would not___

2. she'll ___she will___

▶ **Verb Tenses/Subject-Verb Agreement**
Circle the correct verb in each pair of parentheses.

Arizona (is, are) the land of sunshine. Although the climate varies with the height of the land, it (is, was) mostly hot and dry. In winter, people (visit, visits) Arizona because of its warm climate.

▶ **Pronoun-Antecedent Agreement**
Above each underlined pronoun, write the correct pronoun.

3. General George Custer fought at Little Big Horn. <u>It</u> and 260 soldiers were killed.
   He

4. Clarence Birdseye is famous for <u>their</u> quick-frozen food processing.
   his

▶ **Intensive, Reflexive, and Demonstrative Pronouns**
Fill in the blank with an intensive or reflexive pronoun.

5. Princess Diana ___herself___ traveled on behalf of many charities.

6. Louis Armstrong formed his own bands ___himself___ at an early age.

▶ **Adjectives and Adverbs**
Circle the adjectives and underline the adverbs.

7. Settlers <u>eagerly</u> rushed into the North Dakota territory in the 1870s despite the (severe) weather.

8. The settlers <u>quickly</u> developed (better) methods of cultivation.

▶ Aim, Purpose, and Audience

Before a writer begins any writing project, it is important to know exactly what her aim, purpose, and audience are.

A writer's **aim** is the message she wants to convey. The aim is closely tied to the writer's purpose for writing. For example, the aim of a writer who publishes an informative article may be writing to raise readers' awareness about an issue. So she is doing more than just *informing* her readers, even though that is her basic purpose for writing.

A writer's **purpose** may be to inform, to explain, to entertain, or to persuade. In some cases, a writer may have more than one purpose.

The **audience** is the people who will read or hear the written product. It's important to know who the audience is as you write. For example, if you are writing for your teacher, you may use different words or a different tone than if you are writing for your best friend.

WRITER'S CRAFT

Practice Read each writing topic below. Tell whether the writer's purpose is to inform, to explain, to entertain, or to persuade.

1. **persuade** _____ why cars should be smaller

2. **explain** _____ how to get to school

3. **inform** _____ quilting bees

4. **entertain** _____ my family's vacation bloopers

▶ Tell the audience what each of these products might be written for. Be as specific as you can. **Answers will vary. Possible answers are shown.**

5. a magazine article about taking care of babies **parents** _____

6. an article about DNA **doctors, researchers, scientists** _____

▶ # Plurals

SPELLING

Plurals are words that mean "more than one."

An *s* can be added to the singular form of a noun to form a plural *(cat becomes cats).*

Add *es* to words that end in *sh*, *ch*, *ss*, *s*, and *x* to form plurals *(bushes, matches, messes, buses, boxes).*

In words that end with consonant-*y*, the *y* is changed to *i* before *es* is added *(baby, babies; cry, cries).*

Conventions Strategy
Write the plural form of the following words.

1. number   **numbers**

2. tax   **taxes**

3. smudge   **smudges**

4. cliff   **cliffs**

5. dollar   **dollars**

6. ferry   **ferries**

7. arrow   **arrows**

8. monkey   **monkeys**

9. leash   **leashes**

10. country   **countries**

Name _____ Date _____

▶ Word Origins

Many words have been shortened by common usage. Often it's more convenient, and more informal, to use a shorter version of a longer word.

The word *gymnasium* is often shortened to gym.

Practice

▶ Use the following words to complete the exercise.

exam	lunch	auto	flu	taxi
plane	photo	fridge	limo	phone

▶ Use the words in the box to write the shortened form of each word.

1. refrigerator **fridge** _____

2. telephone **phone** _____

3. automobile **auto** _____

4. limousine **limo** _____

5. examination **exam** _____

6. luncheon **lunch** _____

7. influenza **flu** _____

8. taxicab **taxi** _____

9. photograph **photo** _____

10. airplane **plane** _____

VOCABULARY

►Comparative and Superlative Adjectives

GRAMMAR AND USAGE

Rule

► Some adjectives are comparative. They compare two nouns. Comparative adjectives often end with -er.

► Some adjectives are superlative. They compare three or more nouns. Superlative adjectives often end with -est.

► Some adjectives use *more* or *most* and do not use an *-er* or *-est* ending.

Practice In the sentences below, write *C* after the sentences that have comparative adjectives, *S* after the ones that have superlative adjectives, and O after the ones that have adjectives that use *more* or *most*. Underline the adjectives in each sentence.

1. A blue whale is <u>bigger</u> than a hummingbird. **C**_____

2. The Douglas fir is the <u>tallest</u> tree in our yard. **S**_____

3. The Australian sea wasp has the <u>most painful</u> sting of all animals. **O**_____

4. Write two sentences using the comparative form of the adjective *cold*.
   Answers will vary but should include the word colder.
   _____

   _____

5. Write two sentences using the superlative form of the adjective *young*.
   Answers will vary but should include the word youngest.
   _____

   _____

Name _____ Date _____

 # Organization of a Narrative Paragraph

A **paragraph** is a group of related sentences that support one main idea. Usually, the first sentence tells the main idea of the paragraph. Other sentences in the paragraph support the main idea.

The supporting sentences can be arranged in **order of time** or **order of impression**.

Order of time tells *when* or in *what order* things happen. Use order of time to inform or instruct the reader.

Signal words help the reader follow the order in which things happen.

Examples: *first, next, then, after, before*

Other signal words help the reader follow when things happen.

Examples: *last week, yesterday, a month ago, tomorrow*

Order of impression organizes the details from most to least important. Think about what makes the strongest impression on you.

Practice

▶ **Underline the words that do *not* show the time or order that things happen.**

<u>Under</u>	Tomorrow	First	<u>Behind</u>
Yesterday	Next	<u>Through</u>	Last
Sunday	After dinner	<u>Although</u>	<u>Over</u>

▶ **Write a short paragraph about an ordinary day in your life. Use time and order words in your paragraph.**

Answer will vary.

_____

_____

▶ Compound Words

A **compound word** is a word that is made of two or more smaller words (*playmate, timetable*).

Prefixes and suffixes are not compound words. (*un• fair, play•ed*)

 Use these words to complete the exercise below.

waterfall	grapevine	sometimes	brainstorm	billboard
earthquake	headache	fireplace	outfit	footprint

SPELLING

Compound Word Strategy
Replace one of the words in each compound word to write a spelling word.

1. somewhere   **sometimes**

2. brainwash   **brainstorm**

3. headstone   **headache**

4. fireman   **fireplace**

5. outdoors   **outfit**

6. waterhole   **waterfall**

7. grapefruit   **grapevine**

8. footpath   **footprint**

9. earthworm   **earthquake**

10. billfold   **billboard**

Name _____ Date _____

►Compound Words

> Many compound words are hyphenated.
>
> *first-class*   *well-done*
>
> Many numbers are also hyphenated compound words.
>
> *forty-five*   *seventy-six*

Practice   **Use these words to complete the exercise below.**

cut	step	ice	smelling	self
handed	blooded	six	good	baby

► **Complete each hyphenated compound word with a word from the box.**

1. sixty- **six**

2. clean- **cut**

3. sweet- **smelling**

4. **self** -defense

5. warm- **blooded**

6. **good** -bye

7. **ice** -skating

8. left- **handed**

9. step-by- **step**

10. **baby** -sit

VOCABULARY

UNIT 4 Survival • **Lesson 2** *Arctic Explorer: The Story of Matthew Henson*

GRAMMAR AND USAGE

▶ Comparative and Superlative Adverbs

Rule

▶ Some adverbs are **comparative.** They compare two verbs. Comparative adverbs often end with *-er*.

▶ Some adverbs are **superlative.** They compare three or more verbs. Superlative adverbs often end with *-est*.

▶ Some adverbs use *more* or *most* and do not use an *-er* or *-est* ending.

Practice

▶ **Look at the following sentences. Write the adverb in the blank.**

1. You can easily find resources on the Internet for your report. __easily__

2. Michelangelo's statue *David* is often admired for its realism. __often__

3. Georgia O'Keefe's artworks are precisely painted. __precisely__

▶**Complete the chart by filling in the missing form of the adverb.**

Adverb	Comparative Adverb	Superlative Adverb
fast	faster	**fastest**
often	**more often**	most often
loudly	more loudly	most loudly
hard	harder	**hardest**

Name _____ Date _____

▶Suspense and Surprise

Suspense is a strong feeling of curiosity about what will happen next.

To build suspense, help the reader picture the scene.

Add sounds:
> The footsteps <u>crunched</u> on the gravel sidewalk.

Use vivid verbs and adjectives.
> The cat <u>leaped</u> <u>out</u> from behind the door and <u>flung</u> herself at the <u>scrawny</u>, <u>trembling</u> stranger.

Help the reader feel what the character feels.
> "I don't recognize you anymore," his mother <u>whispered shakily</u>. "You do everything *they* say."

Surprise is the reader's strong reaction to unexpected events.

Practice

1. Write a paragraph creating suspense about the contents of an unopened box. **Answers will vary.**

2. Write a paragraph creating suspense about whether the last batter in the baseball game will hit a homerun or strike out. **Answers will vary.**

3. Write a paragraph that creates suspense as you wait to get your report card. **Answers will vary.**

4. Choose one of the paragraphs you just wrote and add a surprise ending. You may have to change the paragraph a little to add surprise to it. **Answers will vary.**

WRITER'S CRAFT

COMPREHENSION

▶ Author's Purpose

Focus Writers have reasons for writing a story in a certain way.

The **author's purpose** is the reason a story is written a certain way. An author's purpose

▶ can be to *inform*, to *explain*, to *entertain*, or to *persuade*.

▶ affects things in the story such as the *details*, *description*, *story events*, and *dialogue*.

An author can have more than one purpose for writing a story.

Practice Look at the following sentences. Write an *X* next to each sentence that informs the reader. Sentences that inform contain facts and information.

1. **X** _____ The car is one of the primary forms of transportation in the United States.

2. _____ The queen, her family, and the entire kingdom lived happily ever after.

3. **X** _____ The cocker spaniel is a type of dog.

4. **X** _____ Mark Twain is the author of many novels and essays.

▶ Look at the following sentences. Write an *X* next to each sentence that explains something. Writing that explains something may describe how something works.

5. **X** _____ To open the door, you must lift the lever and push.

6. _____ Most children like orange juice.

7. **X** _____ Humans use their teeth to grind food in their mouths.

8. _____ Chocolate cake is everyone's favorite.

▶ **Author's Purpose**

▶ **Look at the following sentences. Write an *X* next to each sentence that entertains the reader. Writing that entertains the reader has story events, dialogue, or details that are sometimes humorous or funny.**

9. _____ We own two horses and three cows.

10. **X** _____ The silly dog laughed until the cows came home.

11. **X** _____ Mickey and the talking frog became good friends.

12. **X** _____ The teacup asked the dish what he thought about Mr. Tibbs.

13. _____ A dictionary lists words in alphabetical order.

▶ **Look at the following sentences. Write an X next to the ones that persuade. Writing that persuades tries to get the reader to think or act a certain way.**

14. **X** _____ You should buy this brand of milk.

15. _____ The boy gave his last cent to charity.

16. _____ The tiger at the zoo looks fierce.

17. _____ They waited in line for hours to buy movie tickets.

18. **X** _____ You must come to dinner tomorrow evening.

Apply

▶ **Write a sentence that informs, explains, entertains, or persuades the reader about the following topics. Answers will vary.**

An animal:_____

A book:_____

A singing mouse:_____

The best dessert:_____

COMPREHENSION

UNIT 4 Survival • **Lesson 3** *McBroom and the Big Wind*

▶ # Abbreviations

An abbreviation is a letter or group of letters that stand for a longer word or phrase: **Sept.** is an abbreviation for **September.** Abbreviations save time, space, and energy when we write.

▶**Use these abbreviations to complete the exercise below.**

Dec.	Feb.	St.	Apr.	Mon.
Nov.	Wed.	Aug.	Mar.	Jan.

SPELLING

Meaning Strategy Complete each sentence with an abbreviation from the box.

1. The work week begins on __Mon.__.

2. The shortest month of the year is __Feb.__.

3. Thanksgiving is in __Nov.__.

4. The first month of the year is __Jan.__.

5. The last month of the year is __Dec.__.

6. I live on Main __St.__.

7. The first of __Apr.__ is April Fool's Day.

8. The third month of the year is __Mar.__.

9. __Aug.__ is a summer month.

10. The middle of the week is on __Wed.__.

▶Personification

Personification is a kind of figurative language. When writers use
personification they give human qualities to things that aren't human.

The <u>door</u> winced in pain as we pounded on it.

The word *door* is being personified.

**Write the name of the object or thing that is being
personified in the sentences.**

1. The sun decided to take the day off.

   sun
   _____

2. The clouds opened up and pelted us with huge raindrops.

   clouds
   _____

3. The pastries in the bakery window were smiling at me.

   pastries
   _____

4. The frightened flowers ran from the meadow when the tornado
   approached.

   flowers
   _____

5. The wind tossed the kite in the sky.

   wind
   _____

VOCABULARY

▶ Conjunctions and Interjections

GRAMMAR AND USAGE

Rule	**Example**
▶ A **coordinating conjunction** connects related groups of words.	▶ **Diego and Marcos** are studying. They are studying **science and math**. Yolanda is here, **but** Sunee is at school.
▶ An **interjection** shows strong feelings and is followed by an exclamation point.	▶ Oh, no**!** The cat is eating the cake!

▶ **Read the paragraph. Circle all the coordinating conjunctions.**

John Glenn was an astronaut (and) a senator. He flew in 1959 in the *Mercury,* (and) he flew in 1962 in the *Friendship 77*. He (and) the *Discovery* crew went into space in 1998 when he was 77 years old.

▶ **Add an exclamation point after each interjection.**

1. Wow**!** Did you see the gymnastics competition in the Olympics?

2. No**!** I didn't take your favorite pen.

3. Oh, no**!** I forgot my homework on the bus.

▶ **Look at the sentences. Make the pair into a compound sentence by adding a comma and the conjunction in parentheses.**

Olga Korbut won many medals in the 1972 and 1976 Olympics. She moved to America in 1991. (and)

Olga Korbut won many medals in the 1972 and 1976

Olympics, and she moved to America in 1991.

UNIT 4 Survival • **Lesson 3** *McBroom and the Big Wind*

▶ Exaggeration

Exaggeration is a way of stretching the truth to add humor or interest to your writing. It takes a statement to an extreme that cannot possibly be true. The reader must be able to recognize it as impossible.

> That guy is so fast he could run around the world in a minute and a half.

Exaggeration is the opposite of literal. Literal is a factual statement.

In most writing, you don't want to use exaggeration too often; it will lose its humor and effectiveness. Tall tales, however, are stories that are all exaggeration, for example, "The Tale of the Fast-Talking Turtle." Turtles don't talk and if they did talk, they probably wouldn't talk fast!

Practice Label each sentence with *E* for Exaggeration or *L* for literal.

E ___ 1. The train was so late we could have walked the 3,000 miles and arrived there faster.

E ___ 2. My dad's shoes are as big as boats—and not just rowboats; I mean ocean liners.

E ___ 3. I was laughing so hard I blew the roof off.

L ___ 4. I was so hungry I had two helpings of spaghetti.

L ___ 5. The redwood tree was the biggest tree I had ever seen.

▶ **Write a tall tale title for each subject. For example, a tall tale about your smart dog might be "The Day My Dog Cooked Dinner" or the "Tale of the Dog Who Cooked for the President."**

1. A big storm ___**Answers will vary.**___

2. A talking parrot ___**Answers will vary.**___

3. A monster in your closet ___**Answers will vary.**___

WRITER'S CRAFT

UNIT 4 Survival • **Lesson 4** *The Big Wave*

►Doubling Final Consonants

Final consonants after short vowels are doubled when suffixes are added to a word.

knot, knotting   *plug, plugged*

Conventions Strategy Complete each sentence with a word from the parentheses.

1. I **knitted** _____ a sweater for my aunt. (knit, knitted)

2. I have a **scar** _____ on my left leg. (scarred, scar)

3. We **mop** _____ the kitchen floor every day. (mopping, mop)

4. I **kissed** _____ my mother goodnight. (kissing, kissed)

5. There was water **dripping** _____ out of the faucet. (drip, dripping)

6. The snake made a **hissing** _____ sound. (hissed, hissing)

7. He **ripped** _____ a page out of his book. (ripped, rip)

8. I went **shopping** _____ last Saturday. (shop, shopping)

9. We **chopped** _____ broccoli for dinner. (chopped, chopping)

10. The audience **clapped** _____ after the play was over. (clap, clapped)

SPELLING

UNIT 4 Survival • **Lesson 4** *The Big Wave*

▶Latin Roots

The words *platform, uniform, transform, reform,* and *inform* contain the Latin root *form.*

The Latin root *form* means "shape."

Oftentimes, knowing the meaning of a root will help you figure out the meanings of unfamiliar words.

Practice Read the following sentences and write the meanings of the underlined words.

1. The president stood on the <u>platform</u> as he read his speech to the crowd.
a raised surface

2. Our <u>uniforms</u> were in great shape at the beginning of the year.
clothing that is the same

3. The decorator will <u>transform</u> the appearance of the hall.
to change in appearance

4. The grinch promised to <u>reform</u> his ways. He will no longer be mean to children.
to make or change for better

5. The principal told us to <u>inform</u> our parents that our school will be closed tomorrow.
to tell

VOCABULARY

Name _____ Date _____

▶ Prepositions

<table>
<tr><th>Rule</th><th>Example</th></tr>
<tr><td>▶ A preposition is a word that relates a noun, pronoun, or group of words to some other word in the sentence. Some prepositions are in, to, for, over, before, and from.

▶ A prepositional phrase is a group of words that begins with a preposition and ends with a noun or pronoun.</td><td>▶ Jane Goodall studied chimpanzees in Africa.

▶ Michael Jordan led the Chicago Bulls to six NBA championships.</td></tr>
</table>

Practice Look at the following groups of words. Write an *X* next to each group of words that is a prepositional phrase.

1. **X** _____ in science class

2. **X** _____ at her desk

3. _____ went home

4. **X** _____ during the 1940s

5. _____ the president spoke

6. **X** _____ at violin practice

7. _____ animals stretched

8. **X** _____ in Italy

9. _____ wash your hands

10. _____ your basic education

11. Write a sentence using the prepositional phrase *at the game.*

Answers will vary. _____

Name _____ Date _____

▶Characterization

> **Characterization** is the way to make a character come alive for your readers.
>
> ### Rule
>
> ▶ Show how the character acts, thinks, speaks, and feels. Also show how other characters respond.
>
> ### Example
>
> ▶ Jameel stopped to move the turtle from the middle of the road. He knew that some drivers didn't even care if they hit an animal. He sang a little song to the turtle as he carried it to the side of the road. As Jameel walked away, he felt relieved that the turtle was safe. His friend Maria teased, "Jameel, you're always saving things."

WRITER'S CRAFT

 Create a character. It could be a person you actually know, a person you make up, or someone you have read about. **Answers will vary.**

How the character acts: _____

How character thinks: _____

How the character speaks: _____

How the character feels: _____

How other characters respond: _____

▶ Author's Point of View

COMPREHENSION

Focus Every story is told from a specific point of view that the author chooses. Point of view may be first-person or third-person.

In writing a story, the author creates a narrator who tells the story from a particular point of view.

▶ In a story told from the **first-person point of view,** the narrator is a character in the story. The narrator uses pronouns such as *I, me,* and *my* when telling the story.

▶ In a story from the **third-person point of view,** the narrator is an outside observer looking at the happenings in the story. The narrator uses pronouns such as *he, she,* and *they* when telling the story.

Practice Look at the sentences below. In the spaces provided, write the point of view of each sentence. Remember, first-person point of view uses pronouns such as *I, me,* and *my*. Third-person point of view uses pronouns such as *he, she,* and *they*.

1. I have three sisters. __first-person__

2. They all have brown hair. __third-person__

3. She is on the volleyball team. __third-person__

4. Caleb told me about his vacation. __first-person__

5. He visited Mount Rushmore. __third-person__

6. My sister lives in San Diego. __first-person__

7. She works for a law firm. __third-person__

8. They will make a decision soon. __third-person__

UNIT 4 Survival • **Lesson 5** *Anne Frank: The Diary of a Young Girl*

▶ **Author's Point of View**

Practice

▶ Fill in the sentences below, using pronouns that show the first-person point of view. Use the pronouns *I, me,* and *my.*

9. I _____ can tell you about the game.

10. Please return my _____ CD as soon as you can.

11. Have you met my _____ mother?

12. He gave me _____ some clues about the mystery.

▶ Fill in the sentences below, using pronouns that show the third-person point of view. Use the pronouns *he, she,* and *they.*

13. He or She _____ likes playing the piano.

14. They _____ are driving across the country next summer.

15. He or She _____ is a college student.

16. She _____ is Raul's youngest sister.

▶ Read the passage below. Then answer the questions.

Delores loves basketball. She reads books about

basketball, she plays basketball wherever and

whenever she can, and she is always asking her friend

Yolanda to play basketball with her. If Dolores can't

play basketball, she imagines winning games.

What is the point of view the passage? third-person _____

Write the word that tells you the point of view. She _____

UNIT 4 Survival • **Lesson 5** *Anne Frank: The Diary of a Young Girl*

►Changing y to i

SPELLING

> The letter *y* is usually changed to *i* in words ending in consonant *-y*.

►**Use these words to complete the exercise below.**

grouchy	thirsty	crazy	dirty	angry
stormy	frosty	windy	hungry	speedy

Conventions Strategy
Write the spelling words that are related to the words below.

1. hungriest   **hungry**

2. dirtier   **dirty**

3. angriest   **angry**

4. speedier   **speedy**

5. grouchier   **grouchy**

6. thirstiest   **thirsty**

7. windier   **windy**

8. crazier   **crazy**

9. stormiest   **stormy**

10. frostiest   **frosty**

Homophones

VOCABULARY

> **Homophones** are words that have the same sound but different meanings and spellings.
>
> The man <u>rode</u> a donkey down the <u>road</u>.
>
> Knowing the meaning of a word is very important when using homophones.
>
> If you do not know the meaning of a homophone, you may use the word incorrectly.
>
> The man <u>road</u> a donkey down the <u>rode</u>. (wrong)

▶ **Use the following homophones to complete the exercise below.**

| soul, sole;   flour, flower;   plain, plane;   tale, tail;   weigh, way |

▶ **Complete each sentence with a homophone from the box.**

1. I grazed the **sole** _____ of my feet against the wall.

2. A tulip is a spring **flower** _____.

3. The passengers boarded the **plane** _____ at 7 p.m.

4. The monkey had a short **tail** _____.

5. The butcher used a scale to **weigh** _____ the meat.

▶ Double Negatives and Contractions

GRAMMAR AND USAGE

Rule	Example
▶ A **contraction** is a single word made of two words that have been combined by omitting letters. Use an apostrophe in place of the omitted letters.	▶ you're (you are) won't (would not)
▶ Don't use two negative words **(double negative)** when only one is needed.	▶ **Incorrect:** I **don't** have **no** CDs. **Correct:** I **don't** have **any** CDs.

Practice

▶ **Write the contraction formed by the words below.**

1. you have **you've**

2. we will **we'll**

3. that is **that's**

4. he is **he's**

5. cannot **can't**

▶ **Rewrite the sentence below so that it does not contain a double negative.**

6. Nobody in our class has seen no comets.

   Nobody in our class has seen any comets.

Double Negatives and Contractions • **Reteach**

▶ Point of View

> **Point of view** answers the question, "Who is telling the story?" Use the same point of view throughout the whole story so readers do not become confused.
>
> **Rule**
>
> **Third-person point of view**
>
> ▶ The narrator is an outside observer and is not part of the action of the story. She uses pronouns such *as he, she, his, her,* and *they* when telling the story.
>
> **First-person point of view**
>
> ▶ The narrator is a character in the story and uses pronouns such as *I, me, my, our,* or *us* when telling the story.

Practice

▶ **Read the following paragraph. Then answer the questions about point of view.**

Carol and Jenny walked down the city street. Both of the girls lived in the city, but they saw the city around them in different ways. Carol said she liked the tall buildings and crowded sidewalks. Jenny said she saw dirt and decay.

1. What point of view did the author use? **third-person**

2. What words tell you the point of view? **they, she**

▶ **Rewrite the paragraph above from Jenny's point of view.**

Carol and I walked down the city street. Both of us lived in

the city, but we saw the city around us in different ways.

Carol said she liked the tall buildings and crowded side-

walks. I said I saw dirt and decay.

▶ Main Idea and Details

Focus The main idea is what a paragraph is about. Details in the paragraph support the main idea.

A paragraph has a main idea and details that support the main idea.

▶ The **main idea** is the most important point the writer makes. The main idea is often stated in a clear topic sentence. The topic sentence is usually at the beginning or the end of a paragraph.

▶ The other sentences in a paragraph have **details,** or information, that describe the main idea more fully.

Practice Look at each of the following groups of main ideas and details. Write an *X* next to the sentence that does not more fully describe the main idea.

1. Main idea: Washington, D.C., became the capital of the United States in 1800.

   ___**X**___ Many cities were named after George Washington.

   _____ It was especially designed to be the capital.

   _____ It was named after George Washington.

2. Main idea: Blind people read with their fingers using Braille, a system of raised dots.

   _____ Braille was developed by Louis Braille in France in 1826 when he was a teenager.

   _____ The Braille alphabet, numbers, punctuation, and speech sounds are represented by 63 different combinations of 6 raised dots arranged in a rectangular shape.

   ___**X**___ I have seen Braille in elevators to represent the floor number.

Main Idea and Details • Reteach

COMPREHENSION

Name _____ Date _____

▶**Main Idea and Details**

▶**Read the following paragraph. Then answer the questions below.**

Birds of prey, also called raptors, are powerful hunters of the sky. There are about 280 different kinds, including eagles, falcons, hawks, owls, and vultures. They all have extremely sharp eyesight. They can spot their prey on the ground from a great height. Raptors have long, strong legs with sharp claws, called talons, for grasping their victims.

Answers will vary. Possible answer are shown.

3. What is this paragraph about? Write the sentence that contains the main idea.

Birds of prey, also called raptors, are powerful hunters

of the sky.

4. Now look for sentences with details that support the main idea. Write one sentence that contains details that describe the main idea more fully.

They can spot their prey on the ground from a great

height.

 **Look at the following paragraph. The main idea is missing. Based on the details in the sentences, write the main idea of this paragraph.**

Food keeps us warm, gives us energy, and helps us grow. Our daily pattern of eating and drinking is called our diet. Lack of the right kinds of food can lead to disease, inadequate growth, and eventually starvation. Eating too much of the wrong kinds of food can cause heart disease and other illnesses.

Answers will vary. Possible answer is shown.

All living things need food.

UNIT 4 Survival • **Lesson 6** *Music and Slavery*

►Review

SPELLING

> **Plurals** are words that mean "more than one."
>
> An *s* can be added to the singular form of a noun to form a plural (*cup* becomes *cups*).
>
> Add *es* to words that end in *sh*, *ch*, *ss*, *s*, and *x* to form plurals (*flushes, catches, passes, buses, foxes*).
>
> In words that end with consonant *-y*, the *y* is changed to *i* before *es* is added (*baby, babies, cry, cries*).

 Conventions Strategy Complete each sentence with a word from the parentheses.

1. I used three **tomatoes** _____ to make my salad. (tomato, tomatoes)

2. I have nine **dollars** _____ in my purse. (dollar, dollars)

3. The dog broke through his **leash** _____ . (leash, leashes)

4. My room **number** _____ is written on my hotel key. (numbers, number)

5. There are many **cabins** _____ in the woods. (cabin, cabins)

6. The baby is twenty-one **inches** _____ long. (inch, inches)

7. The **monkey** _____ ate his banana quietly. (monkey, monkeys)

8. There are over twenty **countries** _____ in the continent of Africa. (country, countries)

9. There are twenty-four **hours** _____ in a day. (hours, hour)

10. I saw an **eagle** _____ in the mountains. (eagles, eagle)

Name _____ Date _____

▶Review

> **Homophones** are words that have the same sound but different meanings and spellings.
>
> Soldiers in the army <u>wear</u> the same uniforms.
>
> <u>Where</u> are the new uniforms we bought yesterday?

Practice

▶ **Use the following homophones to complete the exercise below.**

whale, wail;   toad, towed;   fare, fair;   heard, herd;   there, their

▶ **Complete each sentence with a homophone from the box.**

1. A **whale** _____ lives in water.

2. The truck **towed** _____ the car away.

3. I rode on the tallest ride at the **falr** _____ .

4. **There** _____ are ten oranges on the table.

5. The **herd** _____ of elephants moved through the forest.

VOCABULARY

▶**Review**

GRAMMAR AND USAGE

In the sentences below, underline the comparative and superlative adjectives and adverbs. In the blank, write *C Adj* for comparative adjective, *S Adj* for superlative adjective, *C Adv* for comparative adverb, or *S Adv* for superlative adverb.

1. The deadly nightshade is one of the <u>most poisonous</u> of all plants.
   S Adj

2. A giant sequoia lives ten times <u>longer</u> than a Ponderosa pine. **C Adv**

Combine the two sentences below by using a conjunction. Add an exclamation point after the interjection.

3. Oh I love reading about dancing. I love reading about music.
   Oh! I love reading about dancing and music.

Underline the prepositional phrase in this sentence. Circle the prepositions.

4. (Throughout) <u>the world</u>, people live where the climate and land are good for producing food.

Rewrite this sentence so that it does not contain a double negative. Form a contraction from the words in bold.

5. Our president **does not** have no beard.
   Our president doesn't have a beard.

▶Mood

> **Mood** is the tone or atmosphere of the story. The mood could be happy, sad, angry, suspenseful, mysterious, exciting, and so on.
>
> Writers create mood through these story details:
> *Events.* What kinds of things keep happening?
> *Setting.* Where does the story take place?
> *Descriptions.* What colors, sounds, or smells are described? How are the characters described?
> *Choice of words.* Is the writer using humor? Exaggeration? Silly metaphors and similes?
> *Character's emotions and reactions.* What are they feeling about the events or the other characters?
> *Dialogue.* What do the characters say and how do they say it?

Practice   **Use these clues to figure out the mood.**

1. *Events:* A girl gets caught in a tornado and lands in a strange world.
   Mood: **Most likely answer: Fear or adventure**

2. *Setting:* A cemetery in the middle of the night with owls hooting and wind howling.
   Mood: **Most likely answer: Mystery**

3. *Choice of words:* peaceful as a sleeping child, quiet as a mouse
   Mood: **Most likely answer: peaceful, happy**

4. *Dialogue:* "I have an idea," the little boy said with a gleam in his eye. "Let's go to the zoo and mimic the monkeys. Let's slither with the snakes. Let's sleep with the sloths."
   Mood: **Most likely answer: Happiness or humor.**

WRITER'S CRAFT

UNIT 5 Communication • **Lesson I** *Messages by the Mile*

▶ Classifying and Categorizing

COMPREHENSION

Focus Classifying items into categories is a useful way of organizing information.

Classifying means putting similar things into groups or categories. A **category** is the name under which things are grouped. For example, *trumpet, violin, guitar,* and *clarinet* can be classified into the category *Musical Instruments*.

Musical Instruments (*Category*)

trumpet	guitar
violin	clarinet

Some items can fit into more than one category.

Musical Instruments	**Stringed Instruments**
violin	violin
guitar	guitar

Practice

▶ Look at the groups of things below. In each group, two things belong to the same category, but one does not. Write an X next to the thing that does not belong with the others.

1. _____ Brazil
   __X__ airplane
   _____ France

2. _____ lemon
   _____ orange
   __X__ triangle

3. _____ daisy
   __X__ whale
   _____ tulip

UNIT5 Communication • **Lesson I** *Messages by the Mile*

►Classifying and Categorizing

► Look at the groups of things below. Choose a category from the box that best fits each group. Write the category in the space provided.

U.S. Presidents	Sports	Shapes	Tools	Buildings

4. baseball   hockey   soccer

    Category: **Sports** _____

5. George Washington   Abraham Lincoln   John F. Kennedy

    Category: **U.S. Presidents** _____

6. skyscraper   house   apartment

    Category: **Buildings** _____

7. hammer   screwdriver   wrench

    Category: **Tools** _____

8. triangle   rectangle   circle

    Category: **Shapes** _____

 List two items under each of the following categories.

Answers will vary. Possible answers are shown.

Oceans	Flowers	Countries
Pacific Ocean	**lilies**	**Nigeria**
Indian Ocean	**roses**	**Japan**

COMPREHENSION

UNIT 5 Communication • **Lesson I** *Messages by the Mile*

▶ Words with *re-* or *un-*

SPELLING

> The prefix *re-* means "again."
>
> The prefix *un-* means "not."
>
> The prefixes *re-* and *un-* can usually be added to base words without changing the base word. (*enter, reenter*)

Use these words to complete the exercise below.

| report | reverse | uncover | unplanned | unbeaten |
| replace | unfair | unfit | review | untamed |

 Convention Strategy Add the prefix *re-* or *un-* to the following words to create spelling words. Rewrite the words on the lines provided.

1. port   **report**

2. view   **review**

3. verse   **reverse**

4. fair   **unfair**

5. fit   **unfit**

6. cover   **uncover**

7. planned   **unplanned**

8. beaten   **unbeaten**

9. place   **replace**

10. tamed   **untamed**

UNIT 5 Communication • **Lesson I** *Messages by the Mile*

▶ Descriptive Words

> **Descriptive words** are adjectives that are used to describe a person, place, thing, or idea.
>
> A giraffe has a <u>long</u> neck.
>
> The word *long* used in the previous sentence is a descriptive word used to describe a giraffe's neck.

VOCABULARY

Practice

▶ **Use these words to complete the exercise below.**

thick	rusty	throbbing	severe	shrill

▶ **Complete each sentence with a descriptive word from the box.**

1. There was a __**severe**__ thunderstorm last night.

2. The __**shrill**__ sound of the whistle could be heard for miles.

3. The stone was very __**thick**__.

4. We cannot use __**rusty**__ nails to build houses.

5. My father had a __**throbbing**__ headache.

Name _____ Date _____

▶Phrases

GRAMMAR AND USAGE

Rule	Example
▶ A **participial phrase** includes a participle and any modifiers or objects. A participle is a verb that acts as an adjective to modify a noun or a pronoun.	▶ *Beginning* **his career as a commercial artist**, Walt Disney went on to create many much-loved cartoon characters.
▶ A **prepositional phrase** begins with a preposition and ends with a noun or a pronoun.	▶ The governor walked *into* **the Statehouse**. ▶ The Civil War lasted *for* **four years**.
▶ An **appositive phrase** includes the appositive and any words that modify it. An appositive describes or explains another noun in the sentence.	▶ Louis Armstrong, **a famous trumpet player**, was often known by his nickname "Satchmo."

Practice Read each sentence. Draw a box around the participial phrases. Underline the prepositional phrases. Circle the appositive phrases.

1. Many types <u>of spacecraft</u> are <u>on display</u> <u>at the Alabama Space and Rocket Center</u>.

2. California's largest city, (Los Angeles,) is home <u>to many interesting sites for visitors</u>.

3. <u>Missouri enjoys a central location</u> and access <u>to waterways,</u> ⎡making it an important crossroads.⎦

4. The Appalachian Mountains extend <u>into Maine</u>.

5. Thomas Edison, (the inventor of many things we use today,) was born <u>in Ohio</u>.

▶ Developing Persuasive Writing

> The purpose of persuasive writing is to convince your readers to think, feel, or act a certain way.
>
> **Persuasive methods**
>
> There are two main methods of writing persuasively.
>
> One method is to support your viewpoint with *facts* and *reasons*.
>
> Another persuasive method is to appeal to the *interests or emotions* of the reader. You need to understand your reader and figure out what they care about. Advertisers often use this method to convince people to buy their products.
>
> The method you choose may depend on who your audience is. Will the particular audience respond better to facts or feelings?

Practice For each subject, decide which persuasive method would be most effective for each audience listed.
Answers may vary.

1. An essay telling why the government should spend money on space travel. Your audience is

   Your teacher ___**facts and reasons**___

   Your Senator ___**facts and reasons**___

2. A letter to the editor telling why your town is the best place to live. Your audience is

   Readers of the local newspaper ___**facts and reasons**___

   Readers of a humor magazine ___**interests or emotions**___

3. An article convincing people cats are better companions than dogs. Your audience is

   People who live with dogs ___**facts and reasons**___

   People who live with cats ___**interests or emotions**___

UNIT 5 Communication • **Lesson 2** *We'll Be Right Back After These Messages*

▶ Fact and Opinion

COMPREHENSION

Focus Writers use facts and opinions to support ideas in their writing.

▶ A **fact** is a statement that can be proven true.
   Chicago is a city in the state of Illinois. (You can prove this statement by finding Chicago on a map of Illinois.)

▶ An **opinion** is what someone feels or believes is true. An opinion cannot be proven true or false.
   Chicago is the best city in the world. (This statement cannot be proven true or false. It is a statement about what someone believes.)

Practice

▶ Read the following sentences. Ask yourself the question, "Can this sentence be proven true?" If it can be proven true, then it is a fact. Write an *X* next to each sentence that is a fact.

1. __X__ Two plus two equals four.

2. _____ The color red is better than yellow.

3. _____ Eggs should be eaten for breakfast only.

4. __X__ An eagle has feathers and wings.

5. __X__ A library is a place where people borrow books.

6. _____ In-line skates are better than bicycles.

7. __X__ Apples are not oranges.

8. __X__ Pure maple syrup is tapped from the maple tree.

9. __X__ A balloon filled with helium floats in the air.

10. _____ The New York Yankees have the greatest baseball players.

▶Fact and Opinion

▶ **Read the following sentences. Ask yourself the question, "Can this sentence be proven true or false?" If it cannot be proven true or false, then it is an opinion. Write an *O* next to each sentence that is an opinion.**

11. _____ Five plus five equals ten.

12. __O__ A shirt with short sleeves is better than one with long sleeves.

13. _____ Mars is the closest planet to Earth.

14. __O__ Socks should always be worn with shoes.

15. _____ Foxes prey on small animals.

16. __O__ Everyone should learn to swim.

17. __O__ Classical music is better than rock music.

18. _____ Whales are mammals.

19. _____ The Mississippi River is the longest river in the United States.

20. __O__ Basketball is a better sport than golf.

▶ **Read the paragraph below. The paragraph has both facts and opinions. Draw one line under the facts. Draw two lines under the opinions.**

   All whales should remain in their natural environment. Whales live in both the Pacific and Atlantic Oceans. They live in groups and communicate with one another. I don't think whales should be captured and separated from their families.

 **What's your opinion about whales? Write a sentence stating your opinion. Answers will vary.**

_____

_____

COMPREHENSION

UNIT 5 Communication • **Lesson 2** *We'll Be Right Back After These Messages*

▶ Words with -tion, -ture, or -ure

The letters *-tion, -ture,* and *-ure* are suffixes.

The /shen/ sound can be spelled *-tion.* The /cher/ sound can be spelled *-ture. -ure* can be pronounced different ways.

Use these words to complete the exercise below.

question	action	failure	measure	furniture
mixture	question	protection	lecture	nature

Visualization Strategy
Circle the words that are spelled correctly.

1. (action)   acshon   actiorn

2. quescion   queshon   (question)

3. (construction) construcshon   construcion

4. furnitiure   (furniture)   funiure

5. (failure)   failore   failyor

6. meazure   measore   (measure)

7. mixtore   mixthure   (mixture)

8. (protection)   protectshon   protectcion

9. natore   (nature)   natiure

10. (lecture)   lector   lecshure

Words with -tion, -ture, or -ure • **Reteach**

▶ Multiple Meanings

Many words have more than one meaning. You will often have to look at the words around a word to figure out which meaning is being used in a particular sentence.

<u>Crib</u> is a small bed for a baby.

<u>Crib</u> is also a small farm building or bin in which grain or corn is kept.

Practice **Look at the underlined word in each question. Then circle the answer that is closest in meaning to the underlined word.**

1. We <u>watched</u> the play from the audience.

   a. A device worn on the wrist to tell time.

   (b.) To look closely.

2. My <u>prime</u> concern was getting home safely

   a. Of the best quality.

   (b.) First or greatest in importance or value.

3. I <u>press</u> my own pants.

   (a.) To iron.

   b. magazines, newspapers.

4. I tried a new <u>brand</u> of soap.

   a. a mark made on the skin of cattle.

   (b.) a kind or make of something.

5. The <u>boom</u> of thunder could be heard miles away.

   (a.) a deep hollow sound.

   b. increase dramatically

VOCABULARY

▶ Clauses

GRAMMAR AND USAGE

Rule	Example
▶ A clause is a group of words that has a subject and a verb. An **adjective clause** tells how many, what kind, or which one. An adjective clause may begin with a relative pronoun (who, whom, whose, that, or which) or where or when.	▶ Many presidents whom I admire were born in Ohio. ▶ Tiger Woods, whose real first name is Eldrick, was born in 1975.
▶ An **adverb clause** tells where, when, why, how, or to what degree. Adverb clauses always begin with a subordinating conjunction.	▶ Before he was president, George W. Bush was governor of Texas. ▶ Little farming can be done in North Africa because it is hot and dry.

Practice Read the sentences. Underline the adjective phrases and circle the adverb clauses.

1. The United States and Canada have formed a free-trade zone, <u>which means that goods sold to each other are not taxed.</u>

2. (Because winters are long and snow is plentiful,) skiing, skating, and ice hockey are popular in Canada.

3. I never knew that Canada was so beautiful (until I visited there last summer.)

4. Mr. West, <u>who is the principal</u>, is in a meeting.

5. Maple syrup <u>that is made in Canada</u> is my favorite syrup.

6. (Whenever I think about hockey,) I remember my trip to Canada.

Name _____ Date _____

 # Avoiding Wordiness

> **Wordiness** means using too many words or using bigger words than you need.
>
> One form of wordiness is **redundancy.** That means repeating the same idea or words.
>
> **Example**
> *Wordy:* Eleanor rode all the way to the top of the building in the elevator and got off at the top floor.
>
> *A better way to say it:* Eleanor rode the elevator to the top floor.
>
> Another form of wordiness is using many words when you need only one.
>
> **Example**
> *Wordy:* Oscar thought the shirt was too large in size.
>
> *A better way to say it:* Oscar thought the shirt was too large.

Practice Rewrite each underlined phrase to eliminate unneeded words.

1. Mr. O'Brien was hired by the <u>Department of Labor Department</u>.
   Department of Labor or Labor Department

2. Emily said she would return <u>at a future time</u>. **In the future**

3. The coat was too <u>heavy in weight</u> to wear in the spring.
   heavy

4. Lester went to the store <u>in order to</u> buy a snack. **to**

5. I thought the chili was <u>of a spicy nature</u>. **spicy**

WRITER'S CRAFT

Name _____ Date _____

▶ Words with *-ly*

SPELLING

> The suffix *-ly* can be added to a word without dropping the final *e* or doubling the final consonant. *(bold, boldly)*

Use these words to complete the exercise below.

gladly	loudly	rarely	barely	proudly
quietly	finally	badly	boldly	quickly

 Meaning Strategy Write the spelling words that match each meaning.

1. with much sound   **loudly**

2. with much happiness   **gladly**

3. not afraid   **boldly**

4. making little or no noise   **quietly**

5. with great pride   **proudly**

6. hardly ever   **rarely**

7. just enough   **barely**

8. reacting rapidly   **quickly**

9. in a bad way   **badly**

10. at last   **finally**

UNIT 5 Communication • **Lesson 3** *Breaking into Print*

▶Derivations

> **Derivations** are words that are derived from, or come from, other languages. The word vitamin comes from a Latin word meaning "life."
>
> **Use the vocabulary words to practice derivations.**
> **nostril**—derived from Latin   meaning "nose and hole"
> **fluid**—derived from Latin   meaning "to flow"
> **language**—derived from Latin   meaning "tongue"
> **biscuit**—derived from French   meaning "a small cake of
>   baked dough"
>
> **glossary**—derived from Latin   meaning "a list of difficult
>   words and their meanings"

VOCABULARY

Practice   **Complete each sentence with a word from the box.**

1. We breathe through our **nostrils** _____.

2. The **fluid** _____ spilled from the glass.

3. We had **biscuits** _____ for lunch.

4. Some books have a **glossary** _____ at the end.

5. In Mexico, people speak the Spanish **language** _____.

UNIT 5 Communication • **Lesson 3** *Breaking into Print*

▶ Direct Objects

Rule	Example
▶ A **direct object** answers the question *what?* or *whom?* after an action verb in sentence.	▶ Hank Aaron scored 755 home runs in his career. ▶ My father really admired him.

Practice Read the sentences. Circle each verb that has a direct object. Write *D* over each direct object. Write *no direct object* on the line if the sentence does not have a direct object.

1. Wind and water (shape) Earth's surface. _____

2. Erosion (causes) some changes on Earth. _____

3. Running water (reshapes) the land. _____

4. Some land is removed. **no direct object**

5. Some land is deposited. **no direct object**

6. Wind (blows) sand against rocks. _____

7. The wind (breaks) small pieces off the rocks. _____

8. Even ice (changes) rocks by breaking them apart. _____

9. Rocks may be hard. **no direct object**

10. But they do not stay the same forever. **no direct object**

11. Write a sentence that has a direct object. **Answers will vary.**

_____

_____

_____

Direct Objects • Reteach

Name _____ Date _____

▶ Structure of a Business Letter

The purpose of a business letter, whether through e-mail or regular mail, is to make a request, offer an opinion, or complain.

In any business letter, get to the point quickly.
Request letters are used to order something or ask for information.

State what you want.

State your appreciation.

Complaint letters let someone know there is a problem and you want it fixed.

State the problem.

State the action you expect them to take to fix the problem.

A letter of concern lets someone know what you think. You might be writing a letter to the editor of a newspaper. You want to influence the readers.

State your opinion.

Give your reasons.

State the action (if any) the reader should take.

Be clear and direct about why you are writing and what, if anything, you want the reader to do in response.

Make sure you include your address and the date in the upper righthand corner.

Close with 'Sincerely,' or Yours truly,' and your name.

WRITER'S CRAFT

On a separate sheet of paper, write a letter of concern to the Commissioner of Parks and Recreation to suggest that the city start an afterschool fishing program. Make sure you include all the parts of a business letter. **Answers will vary.**

UNIT 5 Communication • **Lesson 4** *Koko's Kitten*

▶ **Words with -*ful* or -*less***

> The suffix -*less* means "without," and the suffix -*ful* means "full of."
>
> The suffixes -*ful* and -**less** can be added to words without the base word changing.

Use these words to complete the exercise below

healthful	painless	sightless	playful	mouthful
hopeless	restless	skillful	careless	respectful

Conventions Strategy Add the suffix -*ful* or -*less* to each word to create a spelling word.

1. sight   **sightless**

2. hope   **hopeless**

3. pain   **painless**

4. care   **careless**

5. rest   **restless**

6. respect   **respectful**

7. play   **playful**

8. mouth   **mouthful**

9. health   **healthful**

10. skill   **skillful**

UNIT 5 Communication • **Lesson 4** *Koko's Kitten*

▶ Homographs

Homographs are words that are spelled the same but have different meanings and, in some cases, different pronunciations.

The judge at the <u>fair</u> made a <u>fair</u> decision.

A <u>fair</u> is a showing of goods.

A <u>fair</u> decision is an honest decision.

Use these words to complete the exercise below.

present	not absent	a gift
sole	type of fish	alone
poker	a rod for stirring fire	a card game
object	a thing	to protest
entrance	delight; charm	a place to enter

VOCABULARY

Write the meaning of the underlined word in the sentence.

1. Everyone stood at the judge's <u>entrance</u>. ___a place to enter___

2. We used the <u>poker</u> to stir the wood in the fire. ___a rod for stirring fire___

3. I was <u>present</u> at the graduation ceremony. ___not absent___

4. We had <u>sole</u> for dinner last night. ___type of fish___

5. The students will <u>object</u> to an increase in homework. ___to protest___

▶ Fragments, Run-On, Rambling, and Awkward Sentences

GRAMMAR AND USAGE

Rule	**Example**
▶ A group of words that is written as a sentence but is missing a subject or a predicate or both is a fragment.	▶ The president of France
▶ A sentence with no punctuation or coordinating conjunction between two independent clauses is a run-on sentence.	▶ Every day we use our senses they help us experience the world.
▶ A rambling sentence strings together many thoughts.	▶ We read about our senses and we asked questions and then we looked through a microscope.
▶ An awkward sentence is a sentence that does not sound or read well.	▶ Being that we use our senses every day we should protect them because they're ours.

Practice Read the sentences. Write *fragment, run-on,* or *rambling* in the blank.

1. Clara Barton was born in Massachusetts and she was educated at home and she worked as a nurse during the Civil War. **rambling** _____

2. Between 1869 and 1873. **fragment** _____

3. She lived in Europe she helped start hospitals during the Franco-Prussian War. **run-on** _____

▶Outlining

WRITER'S CRAFT

An **outline** is the plan writers use to organize their ideas and notes before they start writing. It is very helpful when you are writing a research paper.

Organize your information into main topics and subtopics. There should be at least two main topics. There should also be at least two subtopics, or none at all, under each level.

Step 1. Write a title for your project.

Step 2. The main headings are numbered with Roman numerals and periods (I. II. III. IV.)

Step 3. Subtopics are indented and labeled with capital letters and periods (A., B., C.)

Step 4. You can break your subtopics into smaller subtopics, which are indented and labeled with Arabic numerals and periods. (1., 2., 3.)

The Disappearance of the Dinosaurs

I. Did they disappear slowly?
   A. Disease
   B. Magnetic reversal
   C. Climate change

      1. Too hot?
      2. Too cold?

II. Did they disappear suddenly?

   A. Supernova explosion
   B. Meteorite

Practice **Choose a topic which you already know a lot about and write an outline for a research paper. You could choose a sport you play, a hobby, an organization you belong to, a historical period, a person you admire or something else. Be sure to include a title. Write your outline on a separate sheet of paper.**

Answers will vary. Make sure students have correctly identified main topics and subtopics and that there are at least two subtopics—or none.

COMPREHENSION

▶ Drawing Conclusions

Focus Drawing conclusions helps readers get more information from a story.

Here is how you **draw conclusions:**

▶ Look for bits of information or details about a character or an event in a story. Use these details to make a statement or draw a conclusion about that character or event.

▶ Sometimes a conclusion is stated in the story. Sometimes it is not. However, a conclusion is always supported by details in the story.

Practice **Read the story. Then answer the following.**

"Mom, do I have to go? Couldn't I stay home?" Alexandra asked when she saw the car drive up. "I don't know how to fish, and I don't want to know. Who wants to touch those slimy things, anyway? And what if I fall off the boat?"

"Alex, honey, don't worry," soothed Mrs. Almeeder. "You'll do fine. Your Uncle Mike is a fine fisherman, and he will show you what you need to know. I'm sure you'll have a great time, if you just give it a chance. Now run along—don't keep Claire and Mike waiting."

Alexandra picked up her lunch bag, put on her cap, and slowly walked out the door.

Several hours later, Alexandra raced into the house. "Mom, Aunt Claire and Uncle Mike are taking the boat out to Hog's Head Bay next week. Uncle Mike says that's the best place for sea bass. They said I can go, if it's okay with you. Please, may I? Please?"

Answers will vary. Possible answers are shown

UNIT 5 Communication • **Lesson 5** *Louis Braille*

▶Drawing Conclusions

1. The story contains many details. One detail is that Alexandra does not know how to fish. Write two more details you find in this story.

Detail: **Alexandra goes fishing with Aunt Claire and Uncle Mike.**

Detail: **Alexandra wants to go fishing next week at Hog's Head Bay.**

2. Judging by the details in the story, what can you conclude?

Alexandra's mother will let her go to Hog's Head Bay.

 **Read the following statement, and draw a conclusion.**

All fish swim.

A trout is a type of fish.

Conclusion: **Trout swim.**

COMPREHENSION

UNIT 5 Communication • **Lesson 5** *Louis Braille*

►Words with ex-

> The prefix **ex-** means "former," "outside," or "outer."

Use these words to complete the exercise below.

experiment	exclaim	excuse	extreme	exception
exhibit	exclude	extend	explore	exchange

Visualization Strategy Write the spelling words that are related to the words below.

1. exceptional   **exception**

2. exchanging   **exchange**

3. exclamation   **exclaim**

4. exploring   **explore**

5. experimental   **experiment**

6. exhibiting   **exhibit**

7. inexcusable   **excuse**

8. excluding   **exclude**

9. extremely   **extreme**

10. extension   **extend**

SPELLING

UNIT 5 Communication • **Lesson 5** *Louis Braille*

▶Simile

> A **simile** is a comparison between two things using the words *like* or *as*.
>
> Example: Jason swims like a fish. Leon is as slow as molasses.

▶ **Use these words to complete the exercise below.**

pie	snow	ice	wink	snail
baby	bird	lion	rock	mouse

▶ **Complete each simile with a word from the box.**

1. as cold as — **ice**

2. as hard as a — **rock**

3. as easy as — **pie**

4. as white as — **snow**

5. as quick as a — **wink**

6. as slow as a — **snail**

7. as quiet as a — **mouse**

8. you'll sleep like a — **baby**

9. as strong as a — **lion**

10. eats like a — **bird**

VOCABULARY

▶ Agreement in Sentences

GRAMMAR AND USAGE

Rule	Example
▶ A singular subject must agree in number with its verb. Singular subjects include nouns and pronouns such as *he*, *she*, and *it*.	▶ The senator votes every week. ▶ She enjoys the symphony.
▶ A plural subject must agree in number with its verb. Plural subjects include nouns and pronouns such as *they* and *we*.	▶ The senators vote every week. ▶ We enjoy the symphony.

Practice Look at the pairs of sentences. Underline the sentence in each pair in which the subject and the verb agree.

1. <u>Muscles help move your body.</u>
   Muscles helps move your body.

2. Your heart are a very important muscle called cardiac muscle.
   <u>Your heart is a very important muscle called cardiac muscle.</u>

3. As it contracts, the heart pump blood to all your body parts.
   <u>As it contracts, the heart pumps blood to all your body parts.</u>

4. Skeletal muscles moves at your command.
   <u>Skeletal muscles move at your command.</u>

▶ **Fill in the correct subject in each sentence. Use the subjects at the end of each sentence.**

5. A third ___**muscle**___ is smooth muscle. (muscle, muscles)

6. Smooth ___**muscles**___ are muscles that work whether you think about them or not. (muscle, muscles)

7. ___**We**___ have different kinds of muscles, all of which are important. (We, He)

UNIT 5 Communication • **Lesson 5** *Louis Braille*

▶ Writing a Bibliography

A **bibliography** is a list of resources about a subject. It includes books, magazines, or other written materials used for research. Writers provide this information so the reader knows where the information came from and where to look for more information.

As you do research for a project, make a note card for each book or article you use. Write the information in this form:

The author's full name (last name, first name, middle initial or name) followed by a period.

The title of the book underlined and followed by a comma.

The name of the publisher, followed by a comma.

The date of publication, followed by a period.

Bakker, Robert T.
The Dinosaur Heresies,
William Morrow, 1986.
New York.

Indent all lines after the first one.

When you put your bibliography together at the end of your paper, put entries in alphabetical order by the last name of the author.

If there is no author's name, list the work alphabetically by title. (If the first word is *The*, *A*, or *An*, use the second word of the title.)

If there is only an editor listed, list alphabetically by editor's last name.

Practice Put these entries in alphabetical order by numbering them from 1 to 3.

__3__ Norman, David. <u>Dinosaur!</u> Prentice Hall, 1991. New York.

__2__ Milne, Antony <u>The Fate of the Dinosaurs.</u> Prism Press, 1991. Great Britain.

__1__ Horner, Jack and Gorman, James. <u>Digging Dinosaurs.</u> Workman Publishing, 1988. New York.

UNIT 5 Communication • **Lesson 6** *My Two Drawings*

►Review

> The prefix *re-* and the suffixes *-ture, -ful,* and *-ly* can be added to words without changing the base word.

Use these words to complete the exercise below.

reward	reverse	adventure	skillful	painful
texture	review	friendly	nature	powerful

 Meaning Strategy Complete each sentence with a word from the box.

1. Sitting is the **reverse** of standing.

2. We should always **review** our notes before an exam.

3. The students got extra recess as a **reward** for good behavior.

4. Sandpaper has a rough **texture**.

5. The mountains, the woods, and the oceans are parts of **nature**.

6. Visiting a zoo can be an **adventure**.

7. This big truck has a **powerful** engine.

8. An artist may be **skillful** at painting portraits.

9. I have a **painful** sore on my left leg.

10. The clown at the circus was very **friendly**.

SPELLING

UNIT 5 Communication • **Lesson 6** *My Two Drawings*

▶Review

> **Homographs** are words that are spelled the same but have different meanings and, in some cases, different pronunciations.
>
> There was a <u>rank</u> odor coming from the <u>rank</u> of garbage bags.
>
> A <u>rank</u> odor is a bad odor.
>
> The <u>rank</u> of garbage bags is a line of garbage bags.
>
> **Use these words to complete the exercise below.**
>
> | | | |
> |---|---|---|
> | **buck** | male deer | a dollar |
> | **lean** | stand slanting | not fat |
> | **meal** | ground grain | food served at a certain time |
> | **palm** | kind of tree | inside of hand |
> | **seal** | a mammal (animal) | a mark of ownership |

VOCABULARY

Write the meaning of the underlined word.

1. A <u>lean</u> piece of meat is healthier than a regular piece of meat.
   not fat

2. Breakfast is the first <u>meal</u> of the day.
   food served at a certain time

3. I have a sore in the <u>palm</u> of my hand.
   inside of hand

4. I saw a <u>seal</u> in the water.
   a mammal

5. I paid a <u>buck</u> for my ice-cream cone.
   a dollar

GRAMMAR AND USAGE

▶Review

▶Phrases

▶ Read each sentence. Draw a box around the participial phrases. Underline the prepositional phrases. Circle the appositive phrases.

1. Maine, (the farthest point east <u>in the United States,</u>) has a rocky coastline.

2. ⬛Containing mountains, lakes, and seashore,⬛ Acadia is New England's only national park.

▶Clauses

▶ Underline the adjective phrase or circle the adverb phrase.

3. Many people <u>who vacation in Rhode Island</u> enjoy swimming, sailing, and fishing.

▶Direct Objects

4. Write a sentence that has a direct object. Circle the direct object.
   Answers will vary. _____

▶Fragments, Run-On, Rambling, and Awkward Sentences

▶ Read the following sentence. Write *fragment, run-on, rambling,* or *awkward* in the blank.

5. Karate contests usually last 2 minutes and are controlled by a referee and four judges and actual physical contact is not necessary to score points. **rambling** _____

Name _____ Date _____

▶ Developing Persuasive Writing

> **Persuasive writing** is used to convince the readers to think, feel, or act a certain way.
>
> ## Persuasive Methods
> One way to persuade the readers is to support your opinion mainly with *facts and reasons*.
>
> If you can't back up your argument with facts and reasons then you can appeal to the readers' *interests or emotions*. You need to understand your readers and figure out what they care about.

Practice

▶ **Do these statements express facts or feelings? Write fact or feeling in the blank.**

feeling 1. Any cat lover would envy you if you had a tiger.

fact 2. Tigers are big cats.

fact 3. Mt. Everest is the tallest mountain in the world.

▶ **Write a paragraph persuading your audience to stop a park from being turned into a parking lot. The parents in your town are your audience. Use an interests and emotions approach.**

Answers will vary.

_____

_____

_____

_____

_____

_____

WRITER'S CRAFT

► Classifying and Categorizing

COMPREHENSION

Focus Classifying items into categories is a useful way of organizing information.

Classifying means putting similar things into groups or categories. A **category** is the name under which the things are grouped.

Kinds of Transportation *(Category)*

horse	airplane
wagon	car

Some items can fit into more than one category.

Kinds of Transportation		**Modern Transportation**	
airplane	car	airplane	car

Practice Look at the groups of things below. All the things belong to the same category except one. Write an *X* next to the thing that does not belong in the same category as the others.

1. _____ broccoli _____ carrot

 _**X**_ oatmeal _____ celery

2. _____ poodle _**X**_ tiger

 _____ cocker spaniel _____ German shepherd

3. _**X**_ hair _____ table

 _____ chair _____ sofa

4. _____ maple tree _**X**_ coat rack

 _____ palm tree _____ oak tree

UNIT 6 A Changing America • **Lesson 1** *Early America*

▶**Classifying and Categorizing**

Look at the groups of things below. Choose a category from the box that best fits each group. Write the category in the space provided.

Clothing	Papers
Colors	Games

5. Category:
checkers
chess
tic-tac-toe

Games _____

6. Category:
hat
shirt
dress

Clothing _____

7. Category:
red
blue
yellow

Colors _____

8. Category:
construction paper
typing paper
tracing paper

Papers _____

Apply List three things for each of the following categories.
Answers will vary.

Movies	Sports	Holidays
_____	_____	_____
_____	_____	_____
_____	_____	_____

COMPREHENSION

UNIT 6 A Changing America • **Lesson 1** *Early America*

▶Rhyming Words

> In **rhyming words** the vowel sound and the letters that follow it usually stay the same, the beginning of the word usually changes.
>
> The words *sum, gum, hum, plum, drum,* and *glum* are words that rhyme.

 Consonant Substitution Substitute the highlighted consonants with those given to you to create words that rhyme with spelling words.

1.	**bl**ob	(s)	slob
2.	**g**rub	(sc)	scrub
3.	**dr**um	(st)	strum
4.	**f**ail	(b)	bail
5.	**h**um	(s)	sum
6.	**ch**ip	(s)	ship
7.	**dr**ip	(t)	trip
8.	**gl**um	(p)	plum
9.	**g**um	(ch)	chum
10.	**p**ail	(m)	mail

▶Classification

> **Classification**: things that are parts of groups.
>
> For example *donkey*, *elephant*, and *zebra* can all be classified as animals.

Classify the following words as fruits or vegetables.

1. apple   **fruit**

2. banana   **fruit**

3. corn   **vegetable**

4. cabbage   **vegetable**

5. orange   **fruit**

6. beans   **vegetable**

7. watermelon   **fruit**

8. peas   **vegetable**

9. strawberry   **fruit**

10. spinach   **vegetable**

VOCABULARY

▶**GRAMMAR AND USAGE**

▶Identifying and Using Parts of Speech

▶Nouns/Plural and Possessive Nouns/Pronouns

Write above each underlined word whether it is a noun (N), a plural noun (PL), a possessive noun (PN), or a pronoun (P).

1. <u>Your</u> <u>body's</u> <u>energy</u> comes from <u>food</u>.
   P   PN   N   N

2. Healthful <u>foods</u> help <u>your</u> <u>body</u> repair itself if <u>you</u> are injured or sick.
              PL   P   N   P

▶Verbs

Read the paragraph. Circle all the verbs.

The sun (is) a 5-billion-year-old star. Light from the sun (arrives) on Earth in 8 minutes. The gravitational attraction between the sun and objects in the solar system (keeps) the objects in orbit. Because Earth (turns) as it (orbits) the sun, the sun (seems) to (move) across the sky during the day.

▶Adjectives

Write three adjectives that describe each noun below.

3. snowboard   _____ _____ **Answers will vary.**

4. football   _____ _____ _____

▶Adverbs

Write an adverb that modifies each verb, adjective, or adverb below.   **Sample answers are shown.**

5. Jake swims ___**well, badly**___.

6. The movie was ___**not, very, too**___ scary.

▶End Rhyme

In many poems, the last words in certain lines rhyme. This is called **end rhyme.** You have heard end rhyme poems since you were a baby. Nursery rhymes use end rhyme.

> Little Jack Horner
> Sat in a corner

There are different end rhyme patterns. In some poems, the last words in the first and second lines rhyme and the last words in the third and fourth lines rhyme. In some poems, only the last words in the second and fourth lines rhyme.

Poets may also use other patterns.

 **Using end rhyme, write your own lines for these familiar verses.**

1.
Humpty Dumpty sat on the wall

Answers will vary. _____

All the king's horses and all the king's men

Answers will vary. _____

2.
Hickory, dickory dock.

Answers will vary. _____

The clock struck one

Answers will vary. _____

Hickory, dickory, dock.

WRITER'S CRAFT

Name _____ Date _____

▶ Internal Rhyme

WRITER'S CRAFT

> **Internal rhyme** is rhyme contained *within* a line instead of at the ends of lines.
>
> **Example**
>> Apples golden and delicious
>> Hung on <u>trees</u>, caught the <u>breeze</u>.

Practice

▶ Put an *X* next to the examples of internal rhyme.

__X__ **1.** Touching cash gives me a bad rash.

__X__ **2.** Whenever I go fishing, I find myself wishing.

_____ **3.** My tiger cat is such a very sweet guy,
And he looks so handsome when he wears his striped tie.

_____ **4.** I think that I am ready for a trip to the moon.

__X__ **5.** I think Teddy and I are ready.

▶ Match the beginning of the sentence in column A with the end of a sentence in column B to create internal rhyme.

Column A

__c__ **1.** It is simply amazing

__d__ **2.** Will the island queen

__b__ **3.** Will the reigning king

__e__ **4.** If you had any common sense

__a__ **5.** I can't go to the show

Column B

a. until the sun is low.

b. sit on the swing?

c. that we are all gazing.

d. want to be seen?

e. you'd stay away from the barbed wire fence.

▶ Making Inferences

 Focus   Making inferences helps a reader understand the total picture in a story.

An **inference** is a statement you make when you read about a character or event in a story.

▶ First, use **information** from the story. Facts and descriptions in a story are types of information you can use to make an inference.

▶ Combine the information from the story with your **personal experience** or knowledge to make an inference.

Practice

▶ **Read the paragraph below. Then answer the questions on this page and the next page.**

When the team got back to the school after the championship game, all their parents and all the students and teachers from the school were there. The crowd had big banners written with the words "Congratulations, Warriors!" Everyone was cheering and waving to them. Some students had decorated their cars with streamers made of crepe paper of the school colors. The principal and the coach gave speeches saying how proud they were of the team. There was a place reserved in the trophy case for their 1ˢᵗ place trophy. A beautifully decorated cake was on the table.

A fact is information you can use to make an inference. In the paragraph above, one fact is that there was a banner saying "Congratulations, Warriors!" Write another fact about the paragraph.

Answers will vary. Possible answers are shown.

The principal and the coach gave speeches saying how

proud they were of the team.

COMPREHENSION

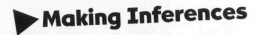

▶ Making Inferences

What do you know? Maybe you have gone to an exciting game. Write something else you know that is related to the characters or events in the paragraph.

Students may attend a school that shows a lot of school

spirit.

Make an inference based on the paragraph on the previous page. To make an inference, use the information from the story and your personal knowledge or experience. Write your inference here.

The team won the championship game.

▶ **Read the following paragraph. Think about the information and your knowledge about the characters and events in the paragraph. Then, complete the inference below with the correct answer.**

Jamie's class had just returned from their field trip to the zoo. They were all talking and laughing about all the exciting and funny animals they had seen. Jamie said, "I loved Bailey, the zoo's newest animal. I was trying to count all his black and white stripes. Guess how many there were."

Inference: What kind of animal is Bailey? **a zebra**

Apply Make another inference from the paragraph above. Write your statement here.

Answers will vary. Possible answer is shown.

Some animals in a zoo are funny.

UNIT 6 A Changing America • **Lesson 2** *The Voyage of the Mayflower*

▶Words with -ing

> The suffix *-ing* means "the act of."
>
> When *-ing* is added to words that end in *e*, the *e* is dropped before adding *-ing*. (*place*, *placing*)
>
> When *-ing* is added to words that end in one consonant + *y*, the final consonant is doubled before adding *-ing*. (*hit*, *hitting*)

 Visualization Strategy Circle the words that are spelled correctly.

1. bikeing (biking)

2. boateng (boating)

3. (building) buildeing

4. (jogging) joging

5. campng (camping)

6. (practicing) practiceing

7. golfeing (golfing)

8. naping (napping)

9. (reading) reaiding

10. exploreing (exploring)

Name _____ Date _____

▶Analogies

VOCABULARY

> An **analogy** is two pairs of words that are related in the same way.
>   **Front** is to **back** as **left** is to **right**.
>
> **Front** is the opposite of **back** and **left** is the opposite of **right**.

Use these words to complete the exercise below.

exit	yes	dry	sell	subtract

1. <u>In</u> is to <u>out</u> as <u>no</u> is to **yes** _____.

2. <u>Win</u> is to <u>lose</u> as <u>buy</u> is to **sell** _____.

3. <u>Lost</u> is to <u>found</u> as <u>enter</u> is to **exit** _____.

4. <u>Near</u> is to <u>far</u> as <u>wet</u> is to **dry** _____.

5. <u>Love</u> is to <u>hate</u> as <u>add</u> is to **subtract** _____.

Analogies • Reteach

Name _____ Date _____

▶ Capitalization and Punctuation

▶ Rewrite the words below using the correct capitalization.

1. april   <u>April</u>

2. thursday   <u>Thursday</u>

3. dr. alvarez   <u>Dr. Alvarez</u>

▶ Capitalization, Periods, and Commas

Use proofreading marks to correct or add capital letters, periods, and commas.

4. california, arizona, and new mexico are states in the southwest united states.

▶ Colons and Parentheses

5. Write a sentence containing a colon or parentheses.
   Idea: We brought these items: pencils, pens, and a ruler.

▶ End Punctuation/Quotation Marks/Underlining

Use proofreading marks to add end punctuation, quotation marks, and underlining.

6. Have you read the book <u>The Velveteen Rabbit</u>?

7. What a great book!

▶ Apostrophes/Hyphens/Semicolons

Use proofreading marks to add apostrophes, hyphens, and semicolons where they are needed.

8. Street signs are important; therefore, carefully watch for them.

MECHANICS

Figurative Language

WRITER'S CRAFT

> **Figurative language** describes one thing by using familiar images associated with something else.
>
> Another term for figurative language is **figures of speech.** There are many figures of speech that can make your writing more interesting.
>
> | **Rule** | **Example** |
> |---|---|
> | ▶ A **simile** uses the word *like* or *as* to compare two things that are not alike. | ▶ The socks in the dryer chased each other around like kids playing tag. |
> | ▶ A **metaphor** compares two things that are not alike without using *like* or *as*. | ▶ The forest fire turned the trees into ghosts. |
> | ▶ **Personification** gives human qualities to an animal, object, or idea. | ▶ My hat refused to stay on my head. |

Practice

▶**Identify each sentence as simile, metaphor, or personification.**

1. The baby was as hungry as a bear waking up from hibernation.
   simile

2. The idea disappeared as quickly as a shooting star. **simile**

3. The flowers bowed their heads against the wind.
   metaphor and/or personification

4. The President was about to enter and the room buzzed in anticipation.
   metaphor

▶ Words with -er or -est

> The ending **-er** means "more" and the ending **-est** means "most."
>
> The base words and the words formed with these two endings are adjectives.
>
> In most cases, *y* changes to *i* when **-er** or **-est** is added to an adjective ending in *y*.   *drowsy*   *drowsier*   *drowsiest*

Conventions Strategy Add the **-est** suffix to the first five words and the **-er** suffix to the last five words.

1. chilly   **chilliest**
2. dirty   **dirtiest**
3. noisy   **noisiest**
4. pretty   **prettiest**
5. healthy   **healthiest**
6. foggy   **foggier**
7. cloudy   **cloudier**
8. creamy   **creamier**
9. fancy   **fancier**
10. gloomy   **gloomier**

SPELLING

►Levels of Specificity

VOCABULARY

An idea related to classification is **levels of specificity.** In classification, *vegetable, vehicle,* and *dog* are general categories, while *carrots, cars,* and *poodles* are more specific items within each category. Ideas can become more specific as you use more specific words to describe them. Each word in the following groups is more specific than the previous one:

food, dessert, pie;
A dessert is a type of food.
A pie is a type of dessert.

►**Use these words to complete the exercise below.**

shark	**golden retriever**	**pianist**	**orange juice**	**hen**

►**Complete each group with a word from the box.**

1. animal, dog, __golden retriever__

2. animal, fish, __shark__

3. fluid, juice, __orange juice__

4. performance artist, musician, __pianist__

5. animal, bird, __hen__

UNIT 6 A Changing America • **Lesson 3** *Pocahontas*

▶ Words, Phrases, and Clauses

▶ Prepositional Phrases

Write an *X* next to each group of words that is a prepositional phrase.

1.   __X__ in Chicago

2.   ___ corn and hogs

▶ Participial, Prepositional, and Appositive Phrases

Read each sentence. Draw a box around the participial phrases. Underline the prepositional phrases. Circle the appositive phrases.

3.   Soil erosion, (the washing or blowing away of topsoil,) happens when trees and plants are cut down.

4.   Food scraps and yard waste have nutrients, making them soil enrichers.

▶ Direct Objects

Circle the direct object in each sentence below.

5.   When skating, Tamara always wears a (helmet.)

6.   You should keep electrical (appliances) away from water.

▶ Adjective and Adverb Clauses

Read the sentences. Underline the adjective clauses and circle the adverb clauses.

7.   I bought a bond, <u>which means that I will get back borrowed money with interest.</u>

8.   (Because people buy less than usual during a recession,) some businesses fail.

GRAMMAR AND USAGE

▶ Alliteration

WRITER'S CRAFT

Alliteration means repeating the consonant sounds at the beginning of words. You have heard it in tongue-twisters:

<u>P</u>eter <u>P</u>iper <u>p</u>icked a <u>p</u>eck of <u>p</u>ickled <u>p</u>eppers.

It is used in poetry. It is also used in advertising!

Practice

I. Write down the sets of alliteration in this verse.

Down by a shining water well
I found a very little dell,
   No higher than my head.
The heather and the gorse about
In summer bloom were coming out,
   Some yellow and some red.

water, well; higher, head, heather; summer, some, some

II. Each of these sayings uses alliteration. Clues are provided to help you finish each saying.

1. Fit as a **fiddle** _____ (*stringed instrument*)

2. Trick or **treat** _____ (*a Halloween greeting*)

3. Hold your **horses** _____ (*an animal you ride*)

4. Copy **cat** _____ (*a kind of house pet*)

III. Write an ad for a food product. Use alliteration to sell the item. For example, Choosy chewers choose Chewy Chocolate Chewing Gum.

Answers will vary.

Name _____ Date _____

▶ Assonance

> **Rule**
> **Assonance** is another term relating to sounds in words. It is the repetition of *vowel sounds* in words. Sometimes it is called *vowel rhyme*. Assonance can make writing smoother and improve the way it sounds when read aloud. It is often used in poetry.
>
> **Examples**
> K<u>ee</u>p your f<u>ee</u>t in the boat. (Long *e* sound is repeated.)
>
> The l<u>i</u>ttle p<u>i</u>gs l<u>i</u>ve <u>i</u>n a house at the foot of the h<u>i</u>ll. (Short *i* sound is repeated.)
>
> With assonance, the words may rhyme (bill, sill) or may just have the same vowel sound (pig, hill).

Practice

▶**Choose the two words in each set that are examples of assonance.**

1. Bed, end, bat, beast   **bed, end**

2. Simple, ring, send, paste.   **simple, ring**

3. Choose, fling, flat, dues   **choose, dues**

4. Purpose, dolphin, awful, raw **awful, raw**

5. Market, dark, light, dim   **market, dark**

▶**Label each set of words as assonance or alliteration.**

Assonance _____ 1. Weather, bell

Alliteration _____ 2. Vote, villain

Assonance _____ 3. Traitor, later

Alliteration _____ 4. Chunky, chilly

WRITER'S CRAFT

►Compare and Contrast

COMPREHENSION

Focus To compare means to tell how things are alike. To contrast means to tell how things are different.

> ► To **compare** means to tell how two or more things are alike.
>   A zebra and a leopard are alike. They are both animals.
>
> ► To **contrast** means to tell how two or more things are different.
>   A zebra and a leopard are different.
>   A zebra has stripes. A leopard has spots.

Practice

►Look at the pairs of words. Write how they are alike in the spaces below.

1. string   rope   **Both are used to tie things.**

2. purse   suitcase   **Both are used to carry things.**

3. car   motorcycle **Both are used for travel.**

4. winter   summer   **Both are seasons.**

►Look at the pairs of words. Write how they are different in the spaces below. **Possible answers are shown.**

5. string   rope   **String is thin. Rope is thick.**

6. purse   suitcase   **A purse is small. A suitcase is large.**

7. car   motorcycle **A car has four wheels. A motorcycle has two wheels.**

8. winter   summer   **Winter is cold. Summer is warm.**

▶**Compare and Contrast**

▶ Look at the pairs of things listed below. Write in the spaces how the things are alike and how they are different.
Possible answers are shown.

Things	Alike	Different
elephant bat	Both are mammals.	An elephant is the largest mammal; a bat is the smallest mammal.
chair desk	Both are furniture.	You sit on a chair. You sit at a desk.
soccer tennis	Both are sports.	In soccer, the ball is kicked through the goal posts; in tennis, the ball is hit over the net with a racket.

Think about two things you might compare and contrast. Write the pair of things in the first column of the list below. In the second column, write how these things are alike. In the third column, write how they are different.

Things	Alike	Different
_____	_____	_____
_____	_____	_____

COMPREHENSION

UNIT 6 A Changing America • **Lesson 4** *Martha Helps the Rebel*

►Latin Roots

SPELLING

> Many English words contain **Latin roots,** or word parts that have meaning. If you know the spellings and meanings of common Latin roots, you can spell and define words that contain Latin roots. The spelling words have these Latin roots:
>
> *fac,* meaning "make" or "do"   *tain,* meaning "hold"
> *mot,* meaning "move"   *port,* meaning "carry"

Use these words to complete the exercise below.

motor	maintain	promote	manufacture	import
factor	satisfaction	obtain	porter	portable

Visualization Strategy Complete the group of letters with a Latin root, to create a spelling word. Rewrite the words on the lines provided.

1. manu^{fact}ure   **manufacture**

2. **fact**or   **factor**

3. satis^{fact}ion   **satisfaction**

4. main **tain**   **maintain**

5. ob **tain**   **obtain**

6. **mot**or   **motor**

7. pro**mot**e   **promote**

8. **port**er   **porter**

9. **port**able   **portable**

10. im**port**   **import**

UNIT 6 A Changing America • **Lesson 4** *Martha Helps the Rebel*

 # Latin Roots

> English words often contain roots from the ancient languages of Greek and Latin. These roots may be found in a variety of words, and have the same meaning no matter where you find them. When you know the meaning of a Latin root, you can begin to figure out the meaning of the English word that contains it. Here are some common Latin roots and affixes and their meanings:
>
> ***trans*** = "across"   ***cred*** = "believe"   ***aud*** = "hear"   ***hosp*** = "host"
> ***anim*** = "life"   ***cap*** = "head"   ***dent*** = "tooth"   ***vis*** = "to see"
>
> The word *dentist* has the Latin root ***dent,*** which means "tooth." You can tell from the meaning of the Latin root that a dentist is a person who takes care of your teeth.

Read each sentence and answer the question below it.

1. The cars were <u>transported</u> from America to Europe by ship.

   What does transported mean? **to carry from one place to another; to move across.**

2. We did not give <u>credit</u> to her story; we thought she was a liar.

   What does credit mean? **belief in the truth of something**

3. The music is barely <u>audible</u>. I can't hear it and neither can the people outside.

   What does audible mean? **loud enough to hear**

4. A birth certificate is a <u>document</u> that lists the day you were born. What is a document? **A printed statement that contains some type of information about something.**

5. Their house is <u>visible</u> from the road. What does visible mean?
   able to be seen

VOCABULARY

GRAMMAR AND USAGE

▶Understanding and Combining Sentences

▶Kinds of Sentences

Write the type of sentence—declarative, interrogative, imperative, or exclamatory—in the space below.

1. Have you ever entered a writing contest? ___interrogative___

2. Some children's magazines have contests for writing poems and stories. ___declarative___

▶Types of Sentences

Write in the blank whether the sentence is a simple sentence or a compound sentence.

3. French and German are the two languages I'm learning.
   ___simple___

▶Coordinating Conjunctions

Join the pair of sentences below into a compound sentence by adding a comma and the conjunction in parentheses.

4. I would like to race motorcycles. My father won't let me. (but)
   I would like to race motorcycles, but my father won't let

   me.

▶Fragments, Run-Ons, Rambling, and Awkward Sentences

Read the sentences. Write *fragment, run-on, rambling,* or *awkward* in the blank.

5. At Dinosaur National Monument. ___fragment___

▶Rhythm

Rhythm in writing is like the beat or pace of music. It is the sound pattern for the words. Rhythm makes your writing pleasing to the ear when read aloud. It also helps to create the mood.

Rhythm is the pattern of accented and unaccented syllables. That means some syllables or words are emphasized more than others. If you did not stress certain words or syllables, your writing would sound boring.

The writer creates the rhythm by his or her choice of words.

Practice Choose two poems you are familiar with. Read them either aloud or to yourself. Then answer the questions. **Answers will vary.**

1. Which poem uses longer words? _____

2. Which poem uses a more simple sentence structure? _____

3. Which poem has a slower rhythm or pace when you read it?

_____ How does the poet create the

slower pace? _____

_____

_____

_____

WRITER'S CRAFT

▶Onomatopoeia

WRITER'S CRAFT

> **Onomatopoeia** is a figure of speech. It is the use of a word that imitates a sound.
>
> **Examples**
> The bell <u>clanged</u>.
> The cow <u>mooed</u>.
> The egg <u>sputtered</u> in the hot pan.
>
> Onomatopoeia can make your writing come alive, especially when you read it aloud. These "sound effects" words help the reader hear the action in your story or poem.

Practice

I. Write a list of sound words you might use to describe car problems.
cough, sputter, chug, sputter, squeal, drip, huff, puff, whir,

buzz, bonk, plunk, achoo, clink, clunk,

II. You are going with your father to talk to the car mechanic about the funny noises the car is making. Help your father tell the mechanic what the car is doing. Use plenty of those sound effects words—that car is in terrible condition.

Answers will vary. Possible answer: The engine chugs and

huffs and puffs when we drive slowly and it whirs and

buzzes and clangs when we drive fast. It sputters and

chatters just before we brake and then it squeaks and

squeals when we stop. The radio coughs the music out. The

air conditioner sizzles and sputters. The steering wheel

clinks, clunks and clatters when you turn it.

▶Sequence

Focus Time and order words help to organize events into logical patterns. Time words help the reader understand when events take place in a story. Order words help the reader to understand in what order things happen in a story.

> Writers often use signal words called **time and order words** to show
>
> ▶ the passage of time in a story. Words such as *Tuesday, tomorrow,* and *the next day* show time.
>
> ▶ the order in which events take place. Words such as *first, then, so, when,* and *finally* show order.

Practice Underline the time and order words in the following sentences.

1. Maria tried to get her homework done <u>before</u> she went to see a movie.

2. At <u>first</u>, she waited in line for her friends.

3. She was reading a magazine <u>when</u> her friends got off the bus.

4. Maria and her friends <u>immediately</u> walked inside the theater.

5. <u>After</u> the movie was over, Maria and her friends went for a walk around the park.

6. <u>Next</u>, Maria went back home to help her parents with dinner.

7. <u>Soon</u> the entire family was sitting around the table.

8. <u>Finally</u>, once dinner was over, Maria went back upstairs to finish her homework.

COMPREHENSION

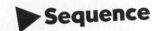 **Sequence**

COMPREHENSION

Use the time words and other words below to correctly complete
the paragraph. Remember to capitalize when necessary.

finally	first	then	after	next

There's a lot to do when making the perfect peanut
butter and jelly sandwich. **First**, you need to decide
what kind of bread is your favorite. Scooping out the
right amount of peanut butter is the **next** thing to
do. **After** that, decide on how much jelly you want
to spread onto the bread. **Then**, grab a napkin so
that you don't make a mess. **Finally**, sit down at the
kitchen table and get ready to eat the perfect peanut
butter and jelly sandwich!

 On a separate sheet of paper, write the events of your
morning using time and order words to make the
sequence of events clear. **Answers will vary.**

▶ Greek Roots

Many English words originated in other languages. Learning the meaning of the **Greek root** will help you discover the meaning of an unfamiliar word.

The Greek root *graph* means "to write." The Greek root *cycl* means "circle."

The Greek root *logy* means "the study of." The Greek root *tele* means "far off."

Use these words to complete the exercise below.

telethon	zoology	telescope	recycle	biology
autograph	geography	bicycle	geology	telegraph

Visualization Strategy Complete each group of letters with a Greek root to create a spelling word.

1. auto**graph**

2. geo**logy**

3. zoo**logy**

4. tele**graph**

5. **tele**thon

6. **tele**scope

7. geo**graph**y

8. re**cycl**e

9. bi**cycl**e

10. bio**logy**

SPELLING

▶Greek Roots

VOCABULARY

English words also contain parts, or roots, that have been borrowed from the ancient language of Greek. When you know the meaning of a Greek root, you can begin to figure out the meaning of the English word that contains it. Here are some common Greek roots and affixes and their meanings. The affixes are circled.

micro = small   *tele* = far off   (*graph* = to write)   *therm* = heat
(*gram* = to write) *log* = word   (*logy* = the study of) *phono* = sounds

The word *telephone* has the Greek roots *tele* and *phon*, which mean "far off" and "sounds." You can tell from the meaning of the Greek roots that a telephone is a device that allows you to hear sounds from far off or far away.

Circle the Greek root in the following words. Then write the meaning of the Greek root next to the word.

1. dialogue   **log means word**

2. microscope   **micro means small**

3. television   **tele means far off**

4. phonograph   **phono means sound**

5. thermostat   **therm means heat**

Name _____ Date _____

▶ Common Irregular Verbs

▶ Verbs

Underline the verbs in the paragraph. Above the verb, write *L* if the verb is a linking verb. Write *H* if the verb is a helping verb. Write *A* if the verb is an action verb.

        L   H   A

Bicycling <u>is</u> a simple traveling method. Bicycles <u>were</u> <u>invented</u> about 200

              L   H   A

years ago. They <u>are</u> inexpensive and <u>do</u> not <u>produce</u> pollution. Bicycles

H A   H   A   A

<u>can</u> <u>go</u> places that cars <u>cannot</u> <u>go</u>. My brother <u>rides</u> his bicycle on the park

             A   L   H

bike trails. He <u>has</u> a racing bike that <u>is</u> very light and fast. <u>Have</u> you ever

A

<u>seen</u> a tandem bicycle?

▶ Verb Tenses

▶ Choose a verb from the box and write it in the space to complete each sentence. Write in the blank at the end of each sentence whether the verb is present, past, or future tense.

include	will play	spoke	live

1. Please **include** your name on your text. **present**

2. I'm sure you **will play** well in the tournament. **future**

3. Martin Luther King, Jr. **spoke** to thousands of people. **past**

4. Some tortoises **live** to more then 100 years old. **present**

▶ Think of an action scene, such as a birthday party or a trip to an amusement park. Then, write a paragraph using the verbs. Use a separate sheet of paper if you need more space.

Answers will vary.

_____

GRAMMAR AND USAGE

▶Repetition

WRITER'S CRAFT

Repetition is the repeated use of words, sounds, or entire lines of poetry. Repetition helps create rhythm in a poem. It also adds emphasis to the idea being expressed.

Example

The <u>rain</u> is <u>falling</u> all around,
    It <u>falls</u> on field and tree,
It <u>rains</u> on the umbrellas here,
    And on the ships at sea.

The poet, Robert Louis Stevenson, repeats the word *rain* and *fall* to help readers see and hear the rain that is falling everywhere.

Practice

Songs often use repetition of entire lines, verses or single words.

     <u>Row, row, row</u> your boat
     Gently down the stream
     <u>Merrily, merrily, merrily, merrily</u>
     Life is but a dream.

Write a short song of your own, repeating words, sounds, or lines. Use the tune from a familiar song, such as "Row Your Boat," or another song.

Answers will vary.

_____

_____

_____

_____

_____

UNIT 6 A Changing America • **Lesson 6** *The California Gold Rush*

▶Review

A **suffix** is a meaningful group of letters that, when added to a base or root word, changes the meaning of the base or root word.

The ending *-er* means "more" and the ending *-est* means "most."

The *-ing* ending means "the act of."

Use these words to complete the exercise below.

dizziest	gloomiest	speediest	curly	climbing
drowsier	fishing	sweatiest	exploring	windiest

 Visualization Strategy Circle the words that are spelled correctly.

1. climbeng   (climbing)

2. (dizziest)   dizzyest

3. drowseir   (drowsier)

4. (gloomiest)   gloomieist

5. windyst   (windiest)

6. (fishing)   fisheng

7. exploreing   (exploring)

8. (curly)   curley

9. (speediest)   speedyiest

10. sweatyiest   (sweatiest)

Name _____ Date _____

▶Review

An idea related to classification is **levels of specificity.** In classification, *vegetable*, *vehicle*, and *dog* are general categories, while *carrots*, *cars*, and *poodles* are more specific items within each category. Ideas can become more specific as you use more specific words to describe them. Each word in the following groups is more specific than the previous one:

fruit, citrus fruit, orange;
A citrus fruit is a fruit.
An orange is a citrus fruit.

▶**Use these words to complete the exercise below.**

watermelon	parrot	corn	chicken	pie

▶**Complete each group of words with a word from the box.**

1. food, dessert, **pie** _____

2. fruit, melon, **watermelon** _____

3. animal, bird, **parrot** _____

4. food, vegetable, **corn** _____

5. food, meat, **chicken** _____

Review • Reteach

Name _____ Date _____

▶Tense

▶Present to Past Tense

Write the past tense of the words listed below.

1. am **was**
2. wonder **wondered**
3. are **were**
4. race **raced**
5. freeze **froze**

6. cook **cooked**
7. make **made**
8. bark **barked**
9. fling **flung**

▶Past to Future

Rewrite the sentences below so that they speak of an action that will happen. **Sample answers are given**

10. Space has been explored. **Space will be explored.**

11. We planted trees on Arbor Day.
   We will plant trees on Arbor Day.

12. Have you ever visited Washington, D.C.?
   Will you visit Washington, D.C.?

13. Many astronauts have made trips into outer space.
   Many astronauts will make trips into outer space.

14. The Chicago Bulls won an NBA championship.
   The Chicago Bulls will win an NBA championship.

15. I have tried to snowboard. **I will try to snowboard.**

GRAMMAR AND USAGE

►Charts, Graphs, and Tables

WRITER'S CRAFT

Charts, graphs and tables are visual presentations of information. Use them to present a lot of information in a small amount of space. They help organize the information so that readers can understand it easily and quickly.

There are many types of charts, tables and graphs you can use. A **pie chart** is a circle that breaks things down into parts of a whole. A **bar graph** compares things or shows how something has changed.

Whatever kind you use, be sure to title it and label the information clearly.

Practice Create a chart that shows how you spend a typical day. Break your day into sleeping, going to school, playing, sports, doing homework, watching television, reading, or any other major activity you do. You can also have a miscellaneous category for small things that don't fit into other categories. Remember, all the activities add up to 24 hours.

Answers will vary. Students should use a pie chart and all parts should add up to 24 hours.

Name _____ Date _____

▶ Details in Descriptive Writing

Make your writing more interesting and vivid with descriptive details that help the reader experience the situation. Tell how things look, feel, taste, sound, or feel. Be specific. Don't just say, "The man looked mean." Tell what made him look mean: "His eyes were cold and his mouth was locked in a sneer."

Practice Rewrite these paragraphs, taking out all descriptive details. Does your new version paint an interesting picture for a reader?

Answers will vary. Possible answers are shown.

1. The small, dark-haired girl in the red hood cheerfully walked through the great oak forest to visit her poor old grandmother. She carried a basket filled with freshly baked bread, strawberry jam and one brilliant red apple.

   The girl walked through the forest to visit her

   grandmother. She was carrying a basket filled with bread,

   jam and one apple.

2. Peter Pan flew quietly yet boldly through the open double window and into the children's room and landed proudly near the bed of a sleeping child. Even after all these years of flying, he was still proud that he could fly. The three children were sound asleep and snoring gently. His companion, a fairy named Tinkerbell, scolded him in a sweet voice like the tinkle of the tiniest of tiny bells.

   Peter Pan flew through the window and into the room and

   landed near the bed. The three children were sound

   asleep. His companion scolded him.

WRITER'S CRAFT

▶Cause and Effect

COMPREHENSION

Focus Cause and effect relationships help readers understand why events happen in a certain way.

> ▶A **cause** is why something happens.
>
> ▶The **effect** is what happens as a result.
>
> | Cause | Effect |
> |---|---|
> | The baby knocked over ——→ | The milk spilled. |
> | a cup of milk. | |
>
> Writers sometimes use signal words to show cause and effect relationships. Signal words such as *because, so, if, then,* and *since* help the reader know what happens and why it happens.

Practice Match each cause in the left column with its effect in the right column. Draw an arrow from the cause to the effect. The first one is done for you.

1. The boy kicked the ball. ——→   **a.** The ball flew through the air.

2. The ice cream bars were left on the kitchen counter.   **b.** Ice cubes are made.

3. An ice cube tray is filled with water and placed in a freezer.   **c.** Dad stepped on the skateboard and broke his ankle.

4. The dog broke the leash.   **d.** The ice cream bars melted.

5. Janet left her skateboard in front of the door.   **e.** A page is printed.

6. The "Print" button is clicked on a computer screen.   **f.** The dog ran wildly through the neighborhood.

7. Vegetables are mashed through a strainer. ——→   **g.** Baby food is made.

Cause and Effect • **Reteach**

Name _____ Date _____

► **Cause and Effect**

Look at the following sentences. Some of the sentences show a cause and effect relationship. Others do not. Write an X next to the sentences that show a cause and effect relationship. Look for signal words such as since, if, so, then, or because. Underline the signal words in the sentences that show cause and effect.

8. **X** Because it is hot outdoors, I will go swimming.

9. ___ The tea is usually served with honey and lemon.

10. ___ Sharon's family will travel to New Mexico.

11. **X** Since he has improved his study skills, Harold has done better on his homework.

12. ___ Jeff forgot to wear his baseball cap.

13. **X** If at first you don't succeed, then try again.

14. ___ Cameron says red cars are faster than blue cars.

15. **X** The pitcher is empty, so someone must have drunk the tea.

16. **X** If you go, then I will, too.

17. ___ The flying saucers filled the skies over Los Angeles.

18. **X** Ted bought Maria a pendant because he likes her.

19. ___ My mother fixed a special lunch for me.

20. ___ We usually go to the movies together.

Apply **Write an effect for the following cause.**

Since Kirsten has a computer, **Answers will vary.**

_____

COMPREHENSION

UNIT 6 A Changing America • **Lesson 7** *The Golden Spike*

▶Review

Learning the meaning of a root will help you decode the meaning of an unfamiliar word that contains that root.
The Greek root **graph** means "to write."
The Greek root **logy** means "the study of."
The Latin root **port** means "to carry."
The Latin root **mot** means "to move."

SPELLING

Use these words to complete the exercise below.

photograph	remote	motor	autograph	geology
technology	bibliography	important	report	biology

Visualization Strategy Complete each group of letters with a Greek or Latin root to create spelling words.

1. auto **graph**

2. biblio **graph** y

3. photo **graph**

4. re **port**

5. im **port** ant

6. re **mot** e

7. **mot** or

8. bio **logy**

9. geo **logy**

10. techno **logy**

Review

> Greek and Latin roots are units of meaning that can be found in the English language.
>
> Some Greek and Latin roots are prefixes and come at the beginning of words. There is a special set of these prefixes that indicate quantity:
>
> **quad** = four   **pent** = five   **hex** = six
> **dec** = ten   **bi** = two
>
> The word *decade* contains the prefix *dec-*, which means "ten." A decade is a period of time equaling ten years. If you know the meaning of a number prefix, you can begin to figure out the meaning of a word with that prefix.

Read the following sentences. Use the underlined word in each sentence to answer the question below it.

1. My cousin from Spain is bilingual. She <u>speaks two languages</u>, Spanish and English.

   What does bilingual mean? **speaking or writing two languages**

2. My apartment is shaped like a pentagon; there is a poster on each of the <u>five sides</u>.

   What does pentagon mean? **A five-sided figure**

3. The barn is shaped like a decagon, there are tools hanging on each of its <u>ten sides</u>.

   What does decagon mean? **A figure having ten sides**

4. The sign is shaped like a hexagon. It has <u>six sides</u>.

   What is a hexagon? **A six-sided figure**

5. My mother gave birth to quadruplets last week. She now has <u>five children</u>.

   What is a quadruplet? **One of four children**

VOCABULARY

UNIT 6 A Changing America • **Lesson 7** *The Golden Spike*

▶Review

GRAMMAR AND USAGE

▶ Capitalization and Punctuation

Read the paragraph. Correct any capitalization or punctuation errors. Use proofreading marks to make the corrections.

<u>d</u>o you like board games<u>?</u>one of my favorite games is <u>monopoly.</u>it was created in the 1930s by <u>charles p.darrow. h</u>e took the names for places in the game from streets in <u>atlantic city, new jersey</u>. What a fun game**!**

▶ Parts of Speech

Read the paragraph. Circle the nouns. Underline the verbs. Draw a box around the pronouns. Make an X on the adjectives, and underline the adverbs twice.

T̶h̶e̶ m̶o̶s̶t̶ v̶i̶o̶l̶e̶n̶t̶ (storms) <u>are</u> (tornadoes). [They] <u>can produce</u> (winds) of 2̶5̶0̶ (miles) per (hour.) (Tornadoes) <u>can form</u> <u>very</u> <u>quickly.</u> (Hurricanes) <u>form</u> over t̶r̶o̶p̶i̶c̶a̶l̶ (oceans.) O̶n̶e̶ of t̶h̶e̶ m̶o̶s̶t̶ d̶e̶s̶t̶r̶u̶c̶t̶i̶v̶e̶ (forces) of X̶ (hurricane) <u>is</u> X̶ s̶t̶o̶r̶m̶ (surge.)

▶ Phrases

Read the sentence. Write *A* over each appositive phrase, *PA* over each participial phrase, and *PR* over each prepositional phrase.

1. The brain, **PA** surrounded by fluid, consists of **PR** billions of **PR** neurons.

▶ Kinds and Types of Sentences

Write simple or compound in the blank to describe the type of sentence. Write *declarative*, *exclamatory*, *interrogative*, or *imperative* to describe the kind of sentence each is.

2. Do you know what a shadow is? **simple, interrogative** _____

Name _____ Date _____

▶ Organization of Descriptive Writing

When you are describing a place, a thing, or even a person, you can use *spatial* order. Spatial order uses *place* or *location* to help the reader see what you are describing. You can arrange your description:

> ▶ From top to bottom
> ▶ From left to right (or vice versa)
> ▶ From inside to outside (or vice versa)

 **Write how each paragraph organizes the information—from left to right, top to bottom or inside to outside.**

1. We made ourselves a super duper ice cream sundae. We started with a banana on the bottom. Then we put three scoops of chocolate ice cream. On top of that we put strawberry syrup, then whipped cream. The chocolate sprinkles covered the top. We crowned it all with six bright red cherries. **bottom to top** _____

2. Emily looked at the drawing of the new playground. If you were standing on Main Street facing the park there would be two basketball courts on the left side, swings and seesaws to the right of the courts, a little playhouse and a little miniature golf course in the center of the playground and a large open field for soccer or baseball on the far right.

left to right _____

WRITER'S CRAFT